MW00649386

THE FLORENCE SCOVEL SHINN'S READER

The Game of Life
Your Word is Your Wand
The Secret Door to Success
The Power of the Spoken Word

CONTENTS

The Game of Life & How to Play It

Chapter 1 - The Game

Most people consider life a battle, but it is not a battle; it is a game.

It is a game, however, which cannot be played successfully without the knowledge of spiritual law, and the Bible offers the rules of the game with wonderful clearness. It may be called the great game of Giving and Receiving.

"Whatsoever a man soweth that shall he also reap." This means that whatever man sends out in word or deed will return to him; whatever he gives, he will receive.

If he gives hate, he will receive hate; if he gives love, he will receive love; if he gives criticism, he will receive criticism; if he lies he will be lied to; if he cheats he will be cheated. We are taught also, that the imaging faculty plays a leading part in the game of life.

"Keep thy heart (or imagination) with all diligence, for out of it are the issues of life." (Prov. 4:23.)

This means that what man images, sooner or later externalizes in his affairs. I know of a man who feared a certain disease. It was a very rare disease and difficult to get, but he pictured it continually and read about it until it manifested in his body and he died - the victim of distorted imagination.

So we see, to play successfully the game of life, we must train the imaging faculty. A person with an imaging faculty trained to image only good, brings into his life "every righteous desire of his heart" - health, wealth, love, friends, perfect self-expression, his highest ideals.

The imagination has been called, "The Scissors of The Mind," and it is ever cutting; cutting, day by day, the pictures man sees there, and sooner or later he meets his own creations in his outer world. To train the imagination successfully, man must understand the workings of his mind. The Greeks said: "Know Thyself."

There are three departments of the mind: the subconscious, conscious and superconscious. The subconscious is simply power without direction. It is like steam or electricity, and it does what it is directed to

9

do; it has no power of induction.

Whatever man feels deeply or imagines clearly is impressed upon the subconscious mind and carried out in minute detail.

For example: A woman I know, when a child, always "made believe" she was a widow. She "dressed up" in black clothes and wore a long black veil, and people thought she was very clever and amusing. She grew up and married a man with whom she was deeply in love. In a short time he died and she wore black and a sweeping veil for many years. The picture of herself as a widow was impressed upon the subconscious mind and in due time worked itself out, regardless of the havoc created.

The conscious mind has been called mortal or carnal mind.

It is the human mind and sees life as it appears to be. It sees death, disaster, sickness, poverty and limitation of every kind, and it impresses the subconscious.

The superconscious mind is the God Mind within each man, and is the realm of perfect ideas.

In it is the "perfect pattern" spoken of by Plato - the "Divine Design," for there is a Divine Design for each person. There is a place that you are to fill that no one else can fill; something you are to do, which no one else can do.

There is a perfect picture of this in the superconscious mind. It usually flashes across the conscious as an unattainable ideal -"something too good to be true."

In reality, it is man's true destiny (or destination) flashed to him from the Infinite Intelligence which is within himself.

Many people, however, are in ignorance of their true destinies and are striving for things and situations which do not belong to them, and would only bring failure and dissatisfaction if attained.

For example: A woman came to me and asked me to "speak the word" that she would marry a certain man with whom she was very much in love. (She called him A.B.) I replied that this would be a violation of

10

spiritual law, but that I would speak the word for the right man, the "divine selection," the man who belonged to her by divine right.

I added, "If A.B. is the right man you can't lose him, and if he isn't, you will receive his equivalent." She saw A.B. frequently, but no headway was made in their friendship. One evening she called and said, "Do you know, for the last week, A.B. hasn't seemed so wonderful to me." I replied, "Maybe he is not the divine selection. Another man may be the right one." Soon after that, she met another man who fell in love with her at once, and who said she was his ideal. In fact, he said all the things that she had always wished A.B. would say to her. She remarked, "It was quite uncanny." She soon returned his love, and lost all interest in A.B.

This shows the law of substitution. A right idea was substituted for a wrong one, therefore there was no loss or sacrifice involved.

The Bible teaches that the Kingdom of God is within man. The Kingdom is the realm of right ideas, or the divine pattern.

The Bible further teaches that man's words play a leading part in the game of life. Many people have brought disaster into their lives through idle words.

For example: A woman once asked me why her life was now one of poverty and limitation. Formerly she had a home, was surrounded by beautiful things and had often tired of the management of her home, and had said repeatedly, "I'm sick and tired of things - I wish I lived in a trunk," and she added, "Today I am living in that trunk." She had spoken herself into a trunk. The subconscious mind has no sense of humor and people often joke themselves into unhappy experiences.

A woman who had a great deal of money joked continually about "getting ready for the poorhouse." In a few years she was almost destitute, having impressed the subconscious mind with a picture of lack and limitation.

Fortunately the law works both ways, and a situation of lack may be changed to one of plenty.

For example: A woman came to me one hot summer's day for a

"treatment" for prosperity. She was worn-out, dejected, and discouraged. She said she possessed just eight dollars in the world. I said, "Good, we'll bless the eight dollars and multiply them," as the Bible teaches that every man had the power to bless and to multiply.

She said, "What shall I do next?"

I replied, "Follow intuition. Have you a 'hunch' to do anything, or to go anywhere?" Intuition means to be taught from within. It is man's unerring guide, and I will deal more fully with its laws in a following Chapter.

The woman replied: "I don't know - I seem to have a 'hunch' to go home; I've just enough money for carfare." Her home was in a distant city and was one of lack and limitation, and the reasoning mind (or intellect) would have said: "Stay in New York and get work and make some money." I replied, "Then go home - never violate a hunch." I spoke the following words for her: Infinite Spirit opens the way for great abundance for ____. She is an irresistible magnet for all that belongs to her by divine right." I told her to repeat it continually also. She left for home immediately. In calling on a woman one day, she linked up with an old friend of her family.

Through this friend, she received thousands of dollars in a most miraculous way. She has said to me often, "Tell people about the woman who came to you with eight dollars and a hunch."

There is always plenty on man's pathway, but it can only be brought into manifestation through desire, faith or the spoken word. Man must make the first move.

Infinite Intelligence, or God, is ever ready to carry out man's smallest or greatest demands. Every desire, uttered or unexpressed, is a demand. We are often startled by having a wish suddenly fulfilled.

For example, one Easter, having seen many beautiful rose-trees in the florists' windows, I wished I would receive one, and for an instant I saw one mentally being carried to the door.

Easter came, and with it a beautiful rose-tree. I thanked my friend the following day, and told her it was just what I had wanted.

She replied, "I didn't send you a rose-tree, I sent you lilies!"

The man had mixed the order, and sent me a rose-tree simply because I had started the law in action, and I had to have a rose-tree.

Nothing stands between man and his highest ideals and every desire of his heart but doubt and fear. When man can "wish without worrying," every desire will be instantly fulfilled.

I will explain more fully in a following Chapter the scientific reason for this and why fear must be erased from the consciousness. It is man's only enemy - fear of lack, fear of failure, fear of sickness, fear of loss and a feeling of insecurity on some plane. We must substitute faith for fear, for fear is only inverted faith; it is faith in evil, instead of faith in good.

The object of the game of life is to see clearly one's good and to obliterate all mental pictures of evil. This must be done by impressing the subconscious mind with a realization of good. A very brilliant man, who has attained great success, told me he had suddenly erased all fear from his consciousness by reading a sign which hung in a room. He saw printed in large letters this statement: "Why worry? It will probably never happen." These words were stamped indelibly upon his subconscious mind, and he has now a firm conviction that only good can come into his life, therefore only good can manifest.

In the following Chapter I will deal with the different methods of impressing the subconscious mind. It is man's faithful servant but one must be careful to give it the right orders. Man has ever a silent listener at his side - his subconscious mind.

Every thought, every word is impressed upon it and carried out in amazing detail. It is like a singer making a record on the sensitive disc of the phonographic plate. Every note and tone of the singer's voice is registered. If he coughs or hesitates, it is registered also. So let us break all the old, bad records in the subconscious mind, the records of our lives which we do not wish to keep, and make new and beautiful ones.

Speak these words aloud, with power and conviction: "I now smash and demolish (by my spoken word) every untrue record in my subconscious

13

mind. They shall return to the dust-heap of their native nothingness, for they came from my own vain imaginings. I now make my perfect records within - records of Health, Wealth, Love and perfect Self-Expression." This is the square of life, The Game completed.

In the following Chapters, I will show how man can change his conditions by changing his words. Any man who does not know the power of the word is behind the times.

"Death and Life are in the power of the tongue." (Prov. 18:21.)

Chapter 2 - The Law of Prosperity

One of the greatest messages given to the race through the scriptures is that God is man's supply and that man can release, through his spoken word, all that belongs to him by divine right. He must, however, have perfect faith in his spoken word.

Isaiah said, "My word shall not return unto me void, but shall accomplish that where it is sent." We know now, that words and thoughts are a tremendous vibratory force, ever molding man's body and affairs.

A woman came to me in great distress and said she was to be sued on the fifteenth of the month for three thousand dollars. She knew no way of getting the money and was in despair.

I told her God was her supply, and that there is a supply for every demand.

So I spoke the word! I gave thanks that the woman would receive three thousand dollars at the right time in the right way. I told her she must have perfect faith, and act her perfect faith. The fifteenth came but no money had materialized.

She called me on the phone and asked what she was to do. I replied, "It is Saturday, so they won't sue you today. Your part is to act rich, thereby showing perfect faith that you will receive it by Monday." She asked me to lunch with her to keep up her courage. When I joined her at a restaurant, I said, "This is no time to economize. Order an expensive luncheon; act as if you have already received the three thousand dollars."

"All things whatsoever ye ask in prayer, believing, ye shall receive." You must act as if you had already received. The next morning she called me on the phone and asked me to stay with her during the day. I said "No, you are divinely protected and God is never too late."

In the evening she phoned again, greatly excited and said, "My dear, a miracle has happened! I was sitting in my room this morning. When the doorbell rang, I said to the maid: 'Don't let anyone in.' The maid however, looked out the window and said, 'It's your cousin with the long white beard.'

So I said, 'Call him back. I would like to see him.' He was just turning the corner, when he heard the maid's voice, and he came back. He talked for about an hour, and just as he was leaving he said, 'Oh, by the way, how are finances?' I told him I needed the money, and he said, "Why, my dear, I will give you three thousand dollars the first of the month."

I didn't like to tell him I was going to be sued. What shall I do? I won't receive it till the first of the month, and I must have it tomorrow. I said, "I'll keep on treating."

I said, "Spirit is never too late. I give thanks she has received the money on the invisible plane and that it manifests on time." The next morning her cousin called her up and said, "Come to my office this morning and I will give you the money." That afternoon, she had three thousand dollars to her credit in the bank, and wrote checks as rapidly as her excitement would permit.

If one asks for success and prepares for failure, he will get the situation he has prepared for. For example: A man came to me asking me to speak the word that a certain debt would be wiped out. I found he spent his time planning what he would say to the man when he did not pay his bill, thereby neutralizing my words. He should have seen himself paying the debt.

We have a wonderful illustration of this in the Bible, relating to the three kings who were in the desert without water for their men and horses. They consulted the prophet Elisha, who gave them this astonishing message:

"Thus saith the Lord - Ye shall not see wind, neither shall ye see rain, yet make this valley full of ditches."

Man must prepare for the thing he has asked for, when there isn't the slightest sign of it in sight.

For example: A woman found it necessary to look for an apartment during the year when there was a great shortage of apartments in New York. It was considered almost an impossibility, and her friends were sorry for her and said, "Isn't it too bad, you'll have to store your furniture and live in a hotel." She replied, "You needn't feel sorry for me, I'm a superman, and I'll get an apartment."

She spoke the words: "Infinite Spirit, open the way for the right apartment." She knew there was a supply for every demand, and that she was "unconditioned," working on the spiritual plane, and that "one with God is a majority."

She had contemplated buying new blankets, when the "tempter," the adverse thought or reasoning mind, suggested, "Don't buy the blankets; perhaps, after all, you won't get an apartment and you will have no use for them." She promptly replied (to herself): "I'll dig my ditches by buying the blankets!" So she prepared for the apartment - acted as though she already had it.

She found one in a miraculous way, and it was given to her although there were over two hundred other applicants. The blankets showed active faith.

Getting into the spiritual swing of things is no easy matter for the average person. The adverse thoughts of doubt and fear surge from the subconscious. They are the "army of the aliens" which must be put to flight. This explains why it is so often, "darkest before the dawn."

A big demonstration is usually preceded by tormenting thoughts.

Having made a statement of high spiritual truth, one challenges the old beliefs in the subconscious and "error is exposed" to be put out. This is the time when one must make his affirmations of truth repeatedly, and rejoice and give thanks that he has already received, "Before ye call I shall answer." This means that "every good and perfect gift" is already man's awaiting his recognition.

Man can only receive what he sees himself receiving.

The children of Israel were told that they could have all the land they could see. This is true of every man. He has only the land within his own mental vision. Every great work, every big accomplishment, has been brought into manifestation through holding to the vision, and often, just before the big achievement comes apparent failure and discouragement.

The children of Israel when they reached the "Promised Land," were afraid to go in, for they said it was filled with giants who made them feel like grasshoppers. "And there we saw the giants and we were in our own sight as grasshoppers." This is almost every man's experience.

However, the one who knows spiritual law is undisturbed by appearance, and rejoices while he is "yet in captivity." That is, he holds to his vision and gives thanks that the end is accomplished, that he has received. So man must ever hold the vision of his journey's end and demand the manifestation of that which he has already received. It may be his perfect, health, love, supply, self-expression, home or friends.

They are all finished and perfect ideas registered in Divine Mind (man's own superconscious mind) and must come through him, not to him.

For example: A man came to me asking for treatments for success. It was imperative that he raise, within a certain time, fifty-thousand dollars for his business. The time limit was almost up when he came to me in despair. No one wanted to invest in his enterprise, and the bank had flatly refused a loan.

I replied: "I suppose you lost your temper while at the bank. You can control any situation if you first control yourself."

"Go back to the bank," I added, "and I will treat." My treatment was:

"You are identified in love with the spirit of everyone connected with the bank. Let the divine idea come out of this situation."

He replied, "Woman, you are talking about an impossibility. Tomorrow is Saturday; the bank closes at twelve, and my train won't get me there until ten, and the time limit is up tomorrow, and anyway they won't do it. It's too late."

I replied, "God doesn't need any time and is never too late. With Him all things are possible." I added, "I don't know anything about business, but I know all about God." He replied: "It all sounds fine when I sit here listening to you, but when I go out it's terrible."

He lived in a distant city, and I did not hear from him for a week, then came a letter. It read: "You were right. I raised the money, and will never again doubt the truth of all that you told me."

I saw him a few weeks later, and I said, "What happened? You evidently had plenty of time, after all." He replied, "My train was late, and I got there just fifteen minutes to twelve. I walked into the bank quietly and said, 'I have come for the loan,' and they gave it to me without a question."

It was the last fifteen minutes of the time allotted to him, and Infinite Spirit was not too late. In this instance the man could never have demonstrated alone. He needed someone to help him hold to the vision. This is what one man can do for another.

One gets too close to his own affairs and becomes doubtful and fearful. The friend or "healer" sees clearly the success, health, or prosperity, and never wavers, because he is not close to the situation. It is much easier to "demonstrate" for someone else than for one's self, so a person should not hesitate to ask for help, if he feels himself wavering.

A keen observer of life once said, "No man can fail, if some one person sees him successful." Such is the power of the vision, and many a great man owed his success to a wife, or sister, or a friend who "believed in him" and held without wavering to the perfect pattern!

18

Chapter 3 - The Power of the Word

A person knowing the power of the word becomes very careful of his conversation. He has only to watch the reaction of his words to know that they do "not return void." Through his spoken word, man is continually making laws for himself.

I knew a man who said, "I always miss a car. It invariably pulls out just as I arrive."

His daughter said: "I always catch a car. It's sure to come just as I get there." This occurred for years. Each had made a separate law for himself, one of failure, one of succes. This is the psychology of superstitions.

The horseshoe or rabbit's foot contains no power, but man's spoken word and belief that it will bring good luck creates expectancy in the subconscious mind, and attracts a "lucky situation." I find however, this will not "work" when man has advanced spiritually and knows a higher law. One cannot turn back, and must put away "graven images."

For example: Two men in my class had had great success in business for several months, when suddenly everything "went to smash." We tried to analyze the situation, and I found, instead of making their affirmations and looking to God for success and prosperity, they had each bought a "lucky monkey." I said: "Oh I see, you have been trusting in the lucky monkeys instead of God. Put away the lucky monkeys and call on the law of forgiveness," for man has power to forgive or neutralize his mistakes.

They decided to throw the lucky monkeys down a coalhole, and all went well again. This does not mean, however, that one should throw away every "lucky" ornament or horseshoe about the house, but he must recognize that the power back of it is the one and only power, God, and that the object simply gives him a feeling of expectancy.

I was with a friend, one day, who was in deep despair. In crossing the street, she picked up a horseshoe. Immediately, she was filled with joy and hope. She said God had sent her the horseshoe in order to keep up her courage.

It was indeed, at that moment, about the only thing that could have registered in her consciousness. Her hope became faith, and she ultimately made a wonderful demonstration. I wish to make the point clear that the men previously mentioned were depending on the monkeys, alone, while this woman recognized the power back of the horseshoe.

I know, in my own case, it took a long while to get out of a belief that a certain thing brought disappointment. If the thing happened, disappointment invariably followed. I found the only way I could make a change in the subconscious was by asserting, "There are not two powers, there is only one power, God, therefore, there are not disappointments, and this thing means a happy surprise." I noticed a change at once, and happy surprises commenced coming my way.

I have a friend who said nothing could induce her to walk under a ladder. I said, "If you are afraid, you are giving in to a belief in two powers, Good and Evil, instead of one. As God is absolute, there can be no opposing power, unless man makes the false of evil for himself. To show you believe in only One Power, God, and that there is no power or reality in evil, walk under the next ladder you see."

Soon after, she went to her bank. She wished to open her box in the safe-deposit vault, and there stood a ladder on her pathway. It was impossible to reach the box without passing under the ladder. She quailed with fear and turned back. She could not face the lion on her pathway. However, when she reached the street, my words rang in her ears and she decided to return and walk under it. It was a big moment in her life, for ladders had held her in bondage for years. She retraced her steps to the vault, and the ladder was no longer there! This so often happens! If one is willing to do a thing he is afraid to do, he does not have to.

It is the law of non-resistance, which is so little understood.

Someone has said that courage contains genius and magic. Face a situation fearlessly, and there is no situation to face; it falls away of its own weight. The explanation is that fear attracted the ladder on the woman's pathway, and fearlessness removed it.

20

Thus the invisible forces are ever working for man who is always "pulling the strings" himself, though he does not know it. Owing to the vibratory power of words, whatever man voices, he begins to attract. People who continually speak of disease, invariably attract it.

After man knows the truth, he cannot be too careful of his words. For example: I have a friend who often says on the phone, "Do come to see me and have an old-fashioned chat." This "old-fashioned chat" means an hour of about five hundred to a thousand destructive words, the principal topics being loss, lack, failure and sickness.

I reply: "No, I thank you. I've had enough old-fashioned chats in my life, they are too expensive, but I will be glad to have a new-fashioned chat, and talk about what we want, not what we don't want." There is an old saying that man only dares use his words for three purposes, to "heal, bless or prosper." What man says of others will be said of him, and what he wishes for another, he is wishing for himself.

"Curses, like chickens, come home to roost." If a man wishes someone "bad luck," he is sure to attract bad luck himself. If he wishes to aid someone to success, he is wishing and aiding himself to success.

The body may be renewed and transformed through the spoken word and clear vision, and disease be completely wiped out of the consciousness. The metaphysician knows that all disease has a mental correspondence, and in order to heal the body one must first "heal the soul."

The soul is the subconscious mind, and it must be "saved" from wrong thinking.

In the twenty-third Psalm, we read: "He restoreth my soul." This means that the subconscious mind or soul must be restored with the right ideas, and the "mystical marriage" is the marriage of the soul and the spirit, or the subconscious and superconscious mind. They must be one. When the subconscious is flooded with the perfect ideas of the superconscious, God and man are one. That is, he is one with the realm of perfect ideas; he is the man made in God's likeness and image (imagination) and is given power and dominion over all created things,

21

his mind, body and affairs.

It is safe to say that all sickness and unhappiness come from the violation of the law of love. A new commandment I give unto you, "Love one another," and in the Game of Life, love or good-will takes every trick.

For example: A woman I know had for years an appearance of a terrible skin disease. The doctors told her it was incurable, and she was in despair. She was on the stage, and she feared she would soon have to give up her profession, and she had no other means of support. She, however, procured a good engagement, and on the opening night, made a great "hit." She received flattering notices from the critics, and was joyful and elated. The next day she received a notice of dismissal. A man in the cast had been jealous of her success and had caused her to be sent away. She felt hatred and resentment taking complete possession of her, and she cried out, "Oh God, don't let me hate that man." That night she worked for hours "in the silence."

She said, "I soon came into a very deep silence. I seemed to be at peace with myself, with the man, and with the whole world. I continued this for two following nights, and on the third day I found I was healed completely of the skin disease!" In asking for love, or good will, she had fulfilled the law, ("for love is the fulfilling of the law") and the disease (which came from subsconscious resentment) was wiped out.

Continual criticism produces rheumatism, as critical, inharmonious thoughts cause unnatural deposits in the blood which settle in the joints.

False growths are caused by jealousy, hatred, unforgiveness, fear, etc. Every disease is caused by a mind not at ease. I said once in my class, "There is no use asking anyone, 'What's the matter with you?' We might just as well say, 'Who's the matter with you?'" Unforgiveness is the most prolific cause of disease. It will harden arteries or liver, and affect the eyesight. In its train are endless ills.

I called on a woman one day who said she was ill from having eaten a poisoned oyster. I replied, "Oh, no, the oyster was harmless, you poisoned the oyster. What's the matter with you?" She answered, "Oh, about nineteen people." She had quarrelled with nineteen people and had become so inharmonious that she attracted the wrong oyster.

Any inharmony on the external, indicates there is mental inharmony. "As the within, so the without."

Man's only enemies are within himself. "And a man's foes shall be they of his own household." Personality is one of the last enemies to be overcome, as this planet is taking its initiation in love. The enlightened man, therefore, endeavors to perfect himself upon his neighbor. His work is with himself, to send out good-will and blessings to every man, and the marvelous thing is that if one blesses a man he has no power to harm him.

For example: A man came to me asking to "treat" for success in business. He was selling machinery, and a rival appeared on the scene with what he proclaimed was a better machine, and my friend feared defeat. I said, "First of all, we must wipe out all fear, and know that God protects your interest, and that the divine idea must come out of the situation. That is, the right machine will be sold, by the right man, to the right man." And I added, "Don't hold one critical thought towards that man. Bless him all day, and be willing not to sell your machine, if it isn't the divine idea." So he went to the meeting, fearless and nonresistant, and blessing the other man. He said the outcome was very remarkable. The other man's machine refused to work, and he sold his without the slightest difficulty.

Good-will produces a great aura of protection about the one who sends it, and "No weapon that is formed against him shall prosper." In other words, love and good-will destroy the enemies with one's self, therefore, one has no enemies on the external!

"There is peace on earth for him who sends good-will to man!"

Chapter 4 - The Law of Non-resistance

Nothing on earth can resist an absolutely non-resistant person.

The Chinese say that water is the most powerful element, because it is perfectly non-resistant. It can wear away a rock, and sweep all before it.

In reality, there is no evil, therefore nothing to resist. Evil has come of man's "vain imagination," or a belief in two powers, good and evil.

There is an old legend that Adam and Eve ate of "Maya the Tree of Illusion," and saw two powers instead of one power, God.

Therefore, evil is a false law man has made for himself through psychoma or soul sleep. Soul sleep means that man's soul has been hypnotized by the race belief (of sin, sickness and death, etc.) which is carnal or mortal thought, and his affairs have out-pictured his illusions.

We have read in a preceding Chapter that man's soul is his subconscious mind, and whatever he feels deeply, good or bad, is outpictured by that faithful servant. His body and affairs show forth what he has been picturing. The sick man has pictured sickness, the poor man, poverty, the rich man, wealth.

People often say, "Why does a little child attract illness, when it is too young even to know what it means?" I answer that children are sensitive and receptive to the thoughts of others about them, and often outpicture the fears of their parents.

I heard a metaphysician once say, "If you do not run your subconscious mind yourself, someone else will run it for you."

Mothers often, unconsciously, attract illness and disaster to their children by continually holding them in thoughts of fear, and watching for symptoms.

For example: A friend asked a woman if her little girl had had the measles. She replied promptly, "Not yet!" This implied that she was expecting the illness, and therefore, preparing the way for what she did not want for herself and child.

However, the man who is centered and established in right thinking, the man who sends out only good-will to his fellow-man, and who is without fear, cannot be touched or influenced by the negative thoughts of others. In fact, he could then receive only good thoughts, as he himself, sends forth only good thoughts.

Resistance is Hell, for it places man in a "state of torment."

A metaphysician once gave me a wonderful recipe for taking every trick in the game of life; it is the acme of non-resistance. He gave it in this way: "At one time in my life, I baptized children, and of course, they had many names. Now I no longer baptize children, but I baptize events, but I give every event the same name. If I have a failure I baptize it success in the name of God!"

In this, we see the great law of transmutation, founded on non-resistance. Through his spoken word, every failure was transmuted into success.

For example: A woman who required money, and who knew the spiritual law of opulence, was thrown continually in a business-way, with a man who made her feel very poor. He talked lack and limitation and she commenced to catch his poverty thoughts, so she disliked him, and blamed him for her failure. She knew in order to demonstrate her supply, she must first feel that she had received - a feeling of opulence must precede its manifestation.

It dawned on her one day that she was resisting the situation, and seeing two powers instead of one. So she blessed the man and baptized the situation "Success!" She affirmed, "As there is only one power, God, this man is here for my good and my prosperity" (just what he did not seem to be there for). Soon after that she met, through this man, a woman who gave her for a service rendered several thousand dollars, and the man moved to a distant city and faded harmoniously from her life.

Make the statement, "Every man is a golden link in the chain of my good," for all men are God in manifestation, awaiting the opportunity given by man, himself, to serve the divine plan of his life.

25

"Bless your enemy, and you rob him of his ammunition." His arrows will be transmuted into blessings.

This law is true of nations as well as individuals. Bless a nation, send love and good-will to every inhabitant, and it is robbed of its power to harm.

Man can only get the right idea of non-resistance through spiritual understanding. My students have often said: "I don't want to be a doormat." I reply "When you use non-resistance with wisdom, no one will ever be able to walk over you."

Another example: One day I was impatiently awaiting an important telephone call. I resisted every call that came in and made no outgoing calls myself, reasoning that it might interfere with the one I was awaiting.

Instead of saying, "Divine ideas never conflict, the call will come at the right time," leaving it to Infinite Intelligence to arrange, I commenced to manage things myself - I made the battle mine, not God's, and remained tense and anxious. The bell did not ring for about an hour, and I glanced at the phone and found the receiver had been off that length of time, and the phone was disconnected. My anxiety, fear and belief in interference had brought on a total eclipse of the telephone. Realizing what I had done, I commenced blessing the situation at once; I baptized it "success" and affirmed, "I cannot lose any call that belongs to me by divine right; I am under grace, and not under law."

A friend rushed out to the nearest telephone, to notify the Company to reconnect. She entered a crowded grocery, but the proprietor left his customers and attended to the call himself. My phone was connected at once, and two minutes later, I received a very important call, and about an hour afterward, the one I had been awaiting.

One's ships come in over a calm sea. So long as man resists a situation, he will have it with him. If he runs away from it, it will run after him.

For example: I repeated this to a woman one day, and she replied, "How true that is! I was unhappy at home, I disliked my mother, who was critical and domineering; so I ran away and was married - but I

26

married my mother, for my husband was exactly like my mother, and I had the same situation to face again."

"Agree with thine adversary quickly." This means, agree that the adverse situation is good, be undisturbed by it, and it falls away of its own weight. "None of these things move me," is a wonderful affirmation.

The inharmonious situation comes from some inharmony within man himself. When there is, in him, no emotional response to an inharmonious situation, it fades away forever from his pathway. So we see man's work is ever with himself.

People have said to me, "Give treatments to change my husband, or my brother." I reply, "No, I will give treatments to change you: when you change, your husband and your brother will change."

One of my students was in the habit of lying. I told her it was a failure method and if she lied, she would be lied to. She replied, "I don't care, I can't possibly get along without lying." One day she was speaking on the phone to a man with whom she was very much in love. She turned to me and said, "I don't trust him, I know he's lying to me." I replied, "Well, you lie yourself, so someone has to lie to you, and you will be sure it will be just the person you want the truth from." Some time after that, I saw her, and she said, "I'm cured of lying."

I questioned: "What cured you?"

She replied: "I have been living with a woman who lied worse than I did!"

One is often cured of his faults by seeing them in others. Life is a mirror, and we find only ourselves reflected in our associates.

Living in the past is a failure method and a violation of spiritual law. Lot's wife looked back and was turned into a pillar of salt.

The robbers of time are the past and the future. Man should bless the past and forget it, if it keeps him in bondage, and bless the future, knowing it has in store for him endless joys, but live fully in the now.

For example: A woman came to me complaining that she had no

money with which to buy Christmas gifts. She said, "Last year was so different; I had plenty of money and gave lovely presents, and this year I have scarcely a cent." I replied, "You will never demonstrate money while you are pathetic and live in the past. Live fully in the now, and get ready to give Christmas presents. Dig your ditches, and the money will come." She exclaimed, "I know what to do! I will buy some tinsel twine, Christmas seals and wrapping paper." I replied, "Do that, and the presents will come and stick themselves to the Christmas seals."

This too, was showing financial fearlessness and faith in God, as the reasoning mind said, "Keep every cent you have, as you are not sure you will get any more." She bought the seals, paper and twine, and a few days before Christmas, received a gift of several hundred dollars. Buying the seals and twine had impressed the subconscious with expectancy, and opened the way for the manifestation of the money. She purchased all the presents in plenty of time.

Man must live suspended in the moment.

"Look well, therefore, to this Day! Such is the salutation of the Dawn."

He must be spiritually alert, ever awaiting his leads, taking advantage of every opportunity.

One day, I said continually (silently), "Infinite Spirit, don't let me miss a trick," and something very important was told to me that evening. It is most necessary to begin the day with right words.

Make an affirmation immediately upon waking. For example: "Thy will be done this day! Today is a day of completion, I give thanks for this perfect day, miracle shall follow miracle and wonders shall never cease."

Make this a habit, and one will see wonders and miracles come into his life.

One morning I picked up a book and read, "Look with wonder at that which is before you!" It seemed to be my message for the day, so I repeated again and again, "Look with wonder at that which is before you." At about noon, a large sum of money was given me, which I had been desiring for a certain purpose.

In a following Chapter, I will give affirmations that I have found most effective. However, one should never use an affirmation unless it is absolutely satisfying and convincing to his own consciousness, and often an affirmation is changed to suit different people.

For example: The following has brought success to many: "I have a wonderful work, in a wonderful way, I give wonderful service, for wonderful pay!"

I gave the first two lines to one of my students, and she added the last two. It made a most powerful statement, as there should always be perfect payment for perfect service, and a rhyme sinks easily into the subconscious. She went about singing it aloud and soon did receive wonderful work in a wonderful way, and gave wonderful service for wonderful   pay.

Another student, a businessman, took it, and changed the word 'work' to business. He repeated, "I have a wonderful business, in a wonderful way, and I give wonderful service for wonderful pay." That afternoon he made a forty-one thousand dollar deal, though there had been no activity in his affairs for months.

Every affirmation must be carefully worded and completely "cover the ground." For example: I knew a woman, who was in great need, and made a demand for work. She received a great deal of work, but was never paid anything. She now knows to add, "wonderful service for wonderful pay."

It is man's divine right to have plenty! More than enough! This is God's idea for man, and when man breaks down the barriers of lack in his own consciousness, the Golden Age will be his, and every righteous desire of his heart fulfilled!

Chapter 5 - The Law of Karma and The Law of Forgiveness

Man receives only that which he gives. The Game of Life is a game of boomerangs. Man's thoughts, deeds and words return to him sooner or later, with astounding accuracy.

This is the law of Karma, which is Sanskrit for "Comeback." "Whatsoever a man soweth, that shall he also reap."

For example: A friend told me this story of herself, illustrating the law. She said, "I make all my Karma on my aunt; whatever I say to her, someone says to me. I am often irritable at home, and one day, said to my aunt, who was talking to me during dinner. 'No more talk, I wish to eat in peace.'

"The following day, I was lunching with a woman with whom I wished to make a great impression. I was talking animatedly, when she said: 'No more talk, I wish to eat in peace!'"

My friend is high in consciousness, so her Karma returns much more quickly than to one on the mental plane.

The more man knows, the more he is responsible for, and a person with a knowledge of Spiritual Law which he does not practice, suffers greatly in consequence. "The fear of the Lord (law) is the beginning of wisdom." If we read the word Lord, law, it will make many passages in the Bible much clearer.

Man can only be what he sees himself to be, and only attain what he sees himself attaining. "Nothing ever happens without an onlooker" is an ancient saying. Man sees first his failure or success, his joy or sorrow, before it swings into visibility from the scenes set in his own imagination. We have observed this in the mother picturing disease for her child, or a woman seeing success for her husband.

So, we see freedom (from all unhappy conditions) comes through knowledge - a knowledge of Spiritual Law.

Obedience precedes authority, and the law obeys man when he obeys the law. The law of electricity must be obeyed before it becomes man's servant. When handled ignorantly, it becomes man's deadly foe. So with the laws of Mind!

For example: A woman with a strong personal will wished she owned a house which belonged to an acquaintance, and she often made mental pictures of herself living in the house. In the course of time, the man died and she moved into the house. Several years afterwards, coming into the knowledge of Spiritual Law, she said to me: "Do you think I had anything to do with that man's death?" I replied: "Yes, your desire was so strong, everything made way for it, but you paid your Karmic debt. Your husband, whom you loved devotedly, died soon after, and the house was a white elephant on your hands for years."

The original owner, however, could not have been affected by her thoughts had he been positive in the truth, nor her husband, but they were both under Karmic law. The woman should have said (feeling the great desire for the house), "Infinite Intelligence, give me the right house, equally as charming as this, the house which is mine by divine right."

The divine selection would have given perfect satisfaction and brought good to all. The divine pattern is the only safe pattern to work by.

Desire is a tremendous force and must be directed in the right channels or chaos ensues.

In demonstrating, the most important step is the first step, to "ask aright." Man should always demand only that which is his by divine right.

To go back to the illustration: Had the woman taken this attitude: "If this house I desire is mine, I cannot lose it; if it is not, give me its equivalent," the man might have decided to move out harmoniously (had it been the divine selection for her) or another house would have been substituted. Anything forced into manifestation through personal will is always "ill-got," and has "ever bad success."

Man is admonished, "My will be done not thine," and the curious thing is, man always gets just what he desires when he does relinquish personal will, thereby enabling Infinite Intelligence to work through

31

him.

"Stand ye still and see the salvation of the Lord" (law).

For example: A woman came to me in great distress. Her daughter had determined to take a very hazardous trip, and the mother was filled with fear. She said she had used every argument, had pointed out the dangers to be encountered, and forbidden her to go, but the daughter became more and more rebellious and determined. I said to the mother, "You are forcing your personal will upon your daughter, which you have no right to do, and your fear of the trip is only attracting it, for man attracts what he fears." I added, "Let go, and take your mental hands off; put it in God's Hands, and use this statement: "I put this situation in the hands of Infinite Love and Wisdom; if this trip is the Divine plan, I bless it and not longer resist, but if it is not divinely planned, I give thanks that it is now dissolved and dissipated."

A day or two after that, her daughter said to her, "Mother, I have given up the trip," and the situation returned to its "native nothingness."

It is learning to "stand still," which seems so difficult for man. I have dealt more fully with this law in the Chapter on non-resistance.

I will give another example of sowing and reaping, which came in the most curious way.

A woman came to me saying she had received a conterfeit twenty-dollar bill, given to her at the bank. She was much disturbed, for she said, "The people at the bank will never acknowledge their mistake."

I replied, "Let us analyze the situation and find out why you attracted it." She thought a few moments and exclaimed: "I know it, I sent a friend a lot of stage money, just for a joke." So the law had sent her some stage money, for it doesn't know anything about jokes.

I said, "Now we will call on the law of forgiveness, and neutralize the situation."

So I said: "Infinite Spirit, we call on the law of forgiveness and give thanks that she is under grace and not under law, and cannot lose this twenty dollars which is hers by divine right."

"Now," I said, "Go back to the bank and tell them, fearlessly, that it was given you there by mistake."

She obeyed, and to her surprise, they apologized and gave her another bill, treating her most courteously.

So knowledge of the Law gives man power to "rub out his mistakes." Man cannot force the external to be what he is not.

If he desires riches, he must be rich first in consciousness.

For example: A woman came to me asking treatment for prosperity. She did not take much interest in her household affairs, and her home was in great disorder.

I said to her, "If you wish to be rich, you much be orderly. All men with great wealth are orderly and order is heaven's first law." I added, "You will never become rich with a burnt match in the pin-cushion."

She had a good sense of humor and commenced immediately, putting her house in order. She rearranged furniture, straightened out bureau drawers, cleaned rugs, and soon made a big financial demonstration - a gift from a relative. The woman herself became made over, and keeps herself keyed-up financially by being ever watchful of the external and expecting prosperity, knowing God is her supply.

Many people are in ignorance of the fact that gifts and things are investments, and that hoarding and saving invariably lead to loss.

"There is that scattereth and yet increaseth; and there is that withholdeth more than is meet, but it tendeth to poverty."

For example: I knew a man who wanted to buy a fur-lined overcoat. He and his wife went to various shops, but there was none he wanted. He said they were all too cheap-looking. At last he was shown one the salesman said was valued at a thousand dollars, but which the manager would sell him for five-hundred dollars, as it was late in the season.

His financial possessions amounted to about seven hundred dollars. The reasoning mind would have said, "You can't afford to spend nearly all you have on a coat," but he was very intuitive and never reasoned.

He turned to his wife and said, "If I get this coat, I'll make a ton of money!" So his wife consented, weakly.

About a month later, he received a ten-thousand-dollar commission. The coat made him feel so rich, it linked him with success and prosperity; without the coat he would not have received the commission. It was an investment paying large dividends!

If man ignores these leadings to spend or to give, the same amount of money will go in an uninteresting or unhappy way.

For example: A woman told me, on Thanksgiving Day, she informed her family that they could not afford a Thanksgiving dinner. She had the money, but decided to save it. A few days later, someone entered her room and took from the bureau drawer the exact amount the dinner would have cost.

The law always stands back of the man who spends fearlessly, with wisdom.

For example: One of my students was shopping with her little nephew. The child clamored for a toy, which she told him she could not afford to buy. She realized suddenly that she was seeking lack, and not recognizing God as her supply! So she bought the toy, and on her way home, picked up, in the street, the exact amount of money she had paid for it.

Man's supply is inexhaustible and unfailing when fully trusted, but faith or trust must precede the demonstration. "According to your faith be it unto you." "Faith is the substance of things hoped for, the evidence of things not seen," for faith holds the vision steady, and the adverse pictures are dissolved and dissipated, and "in due season we shall reap, if we faint not."

The law of grace, or forgiveness, is the law which frees man from the law of cause and effect - the law of consequence. "Under grace, and not under law."

We are told that on this plane, man reaps where he has not sown; the gifts of God are simply poured out upon him. "All that the Kingdom affords is his." This continued state of bliss awaits the man who has overcome the race (or world) thought.

Chapter 6 - Casting the Burden - Impressing the Subconscious

When man knows his own powers and the workings of his mind, his great desire is to find an easy and quick way to impress the subconscious with good, for simply an intellectual knowledge of the Truth will not bring results.

In my own case, I found the easiest way is in "casting the burden."

A metaphysician once explained it in this manner. He said, "The only thing which gives anything weight in nature is the law of gravitation, and if a boulder could be taken high above the planet, there would be no weight in that boulder."

We are also told in the fifty-fifth Psalm, to "cast thy burden upon the Lord." Many passages in the Bible state that the battle is God's not man's and that man is always to "stand still" and see the Salvation of the Lord.

This indicates that the superconscious mind (or God within) is the department which fights man's battle and relieves him of burdens.

We see, therefore, that man violates law if he carries a burden, and a burden is an adverse thought or condition, and this thought or condition has its root in the subconscious. It seems almost impossible to make any headway directing the subconscious from the conscious, or reasoning mind, as the reasoning mind (the intellect) is limited in its conceptions, and filled with doubts and fears. How scientific it then is to cast the burden upon the superconscious mind (or God within) where it is "made light," or dissolved into its native nothingness.

For example: A woman in urgent need of money, "made light" upon the superconscious with the statement, "I cast this burden of lack on the God (within) and I go free to have plenty!"

The belief in lack was her burden, and as she cast it upon the Superconscious with its belief of plenty. An avalanche of supply was the result.

Another example: One of my students had been given a new piano, and there was no room in her studio for it until she had moved out the old one. She was in a state of perplexity. She wanted to keep the old piano, but knew of no place to send it. She became desperate, as the new piano was to be sent immediately; in fact, was on its way, with no place to put it. She said it came to her to repeat, "I cast this burden on the God within, and I go free."

A few moments later, her phone rang, and a woman friend asked if she might rent her old piano, and it was moved out, a few minutes before the new one arrived.

I knew a woman whose burden was resentment. She said, "I cast this burden of resentment on the God within, and I go free, to be loving, harmonious and happy." The Almighty superconscious flooded the subconscious with love, and her whole life was changed. For years, resentment had held her in a state of torment and imprisoned her soul (the subconscious mind).

The statement should be made over and over and over, sometimes for hours at a time, silently or audibly, with quietness but determination. I have often compared it to winding-up a victrola. We must wind ourselves up with spoken words.

I have noticed, in "casting the burden," after a little while, one seems to see clearly. It is impossible to have clear vision while in the throes of carnal mind. Doubts and fear poison the mind and body and imagination runs riot, attracting disaster and disease.

In steadily repeating the affirmation, "I cast this burden on the God within, and go free," the vision clears, and with it a feeling of relief, and sooner or later comes the manifestation of good, be it health, happiness or supply.

One of my students once asked me to explain the "darkness before the dawn." I referred in a preceding Chapter to the fact that often, before the big demonstration, "everything seems to go wrong," and deep depression clouds the consciousness. It means that out of the subconscious are rising the doubts and fears of the ages. These old derelicts of the subconscious rise to the surface, to be put out.

It is then that man should clap his cymbals, like Jehoshaphat, and give thanks that he is saved, even though he seems surrounded by the enemy (the situation of lack or disease). The student continued, "How long must one remain in the dark?" and I replied, "Until one can see in the dark, and casting the burden enables one to see in the dark."

In order to impress the subconscious, active faith is always essential. "Faith without works is dead." In these Chapters I have endeavored to bring out this point.

I will give another example showing how necessary this step is. In fact, active faith is the bridge over which man passes to his Promised Land.

Through misunderstanding, a woman had been separated from her husband whom she love deeply. He refused all offers of reconciliation and would not communicate with her in any way. Coming into the knowledge of Spiritual law, she denied the appearance of separation. She made this statement: "There is no separation in Divine Mind, therefore, I cannot be separated from the love and companionship which are mine by divine right."

She showed active faith by arranging a place for him at the table every day, thereby impressing the subconscious with a picture of his return. Over a year passed, but she never wavered, and one day he walked in.

The subconscious is often impressed through music. Music has a fourth dimensional quality and releases the soul from imprisonment. It makes wonderful things seem possible and easy of accomplishment!

I have a friend who uses her victrola daily for this purpose. It puts her in perfect harmony and releases the imagination. Another woman often dances while making her affirmations. The rhythm and harmony of music and motion carry her words forth with tremendous power.

The student must remember also, not to despise the "day of small things." Invariably, before a demonstration, come "signs of land."

Before Columbus reached America, he saw birds and twigs which showed him land was near. So it is with a demonstration; but often the student mistakes it for the demonstration itself, and is disappointed.

For example: A woman had "spoken the word" for a set of dishes. Not long afterwards a friend gave her a dish which was old and cracked. She came to me and said, "Well, I asked for a set of dishes, and all I got was a cracked plate." I replied, "The plate was only signs of land. It shows your dishes are coming - look upon it as a birds and seaweed," and not long afterwards the dishes came.

Continually "making-believe," impresses the subconscious. If one makes believe he is rich, and makes believe he is successful, in "due time he will reap."

For example: I know of a woman who was very poor, but no one could make her feel poor. She earned a small amount of money from rich friends, who constantly reminded her of her poverty, and to be careful and saving. Regardless of their admonitions, she would spend all her earnings on a hat, or make someone a gift, and be in a rapturous state of mind. Her thoughts were always centered on beautiful clothes and "rings and things," but without envying others.

She lived in the world of the wondrous, and only riches seemed real to her. Before long she married a rich man, and the rings and things became visible. I do not know whether the man was the "Divine Selection," but opulence had to manifest in her life, as she had imaged only opulence.

There is no peace or happiness for man until he has erased all fear from the subconscious. Fear is misdirected energy and must be redirected, or transmuted into Faith.

I am asked, so often by my students, "How can I get rid of fear?"

I reply, "By walking up to the thing you are afraid of."

"The lion takes its fierceness from your fear." Walk up to the lion, and he will disappear; run away and he runs after you.

I have shown in previous Chapters how the lion of lack disappeared when the individual spent money fearlessly, showing faith that God was his supply and therefore, unfailing. Many of my students have come out of the bondage of poverty, and are now bountifully supplied through losing all fear of letting money go out. The subconscious is impressed with the truth that God is the Giver and Gift; therefore as one is one with the Giver, he is one with the Gift. A splendid statement is, "I now thank God the Giver for God the Gift."

Man has so long separated himself from his good and his supply through thoughts of separation and lack, that sometimes it takes dynamite to dislodge these false ideas from the subconscious, and the dynamite is a big situation.

We see in the foregoing illustration how the individual was freed from his bondage by showing fearlessness. Man should watch himself hourly to detect if his motive for action is fear or faith.

"Choose ye this day whom we shall serve," fear or faith.

Perhaps one's fear is of personality. Then do not avoid the people feared; be willing to meet them cheerfully, and they will either prove "golden links in the chain of one's good," or disappear harmoniously from one's pathway.

Perhaps one's fear is of disease or germs. Then one should be fearless and undisturbed in a germ-laden situation, and he would be immune. One can only contract germs while vibrating at the same rate as the germ, and fear drags men down to the level of the germ. Of course, the disease-laden germ is the product of carnal mind, as all thought must objectify. Germs do not exist in the superconscious or Divine Mind, therefore are the product of man's "vain imagination."

"In the twinkling of an eye," man's release will come when he realizes there is no power in evil. The material world will fade away, and the fourth dimensional world, the "World of the Wondrous," will swing into manifestation.

"And I saw a new heaven, and a new earth - and there shall be no more death, neither sorrow nor crying, neither shall there be any more pain; for the former things are passed away."

Chapter 7 - Love

Every man on this planet is taking his initiation in love. "A new commandment I give unto you, that ye love one another." Ouspensky states, in "Tertium Organum," that "love is a cosmic phenomenon," and opens to man the fourth dimensional world, "The World of the Wondrous."

Real love is selfless and free from fear. It pours itself out upon the object of its affection without demanding any return. Its joy is in the joy of giving. Love is God in manifestation and the strongest magnetic force in the universe. Pure, unselfish love draws to itself its own; it does not need to seek or demand. Scarcely anyone has the faintest conception of real love. Man is selfish, tyrannical or fearful in his affections, thereby losing the thing he loves. Jealousy is the worst enemy of love, for the imagination runs riot, seeing the loved one attracted to another, and invariably these fears objectify if they are not neutralized.

For example: A woman came to me in deep distress. The man she loved had left her for other women, and said he never intended to marry her. She was torn with jealousy and resentment and said she hoped he would suffer as he had made her suffer, and added, "How could he leave me when I loved him so much?"

I replied, "You are not loving that man, you are hating him," and added, "You can never receive what you have never given. Give a perfect love and you will receive a perfect love. Perfect yourself on this man. Give him a perfect, unselfish love, demanding nothing in return, do not criticise or condemn, and bless him wherever his is."

She replied, "No, I won't bless him unless I know where he is!" she said.

"Well," I said, "that is not real love."

"When you send out real love, real love will return to you, either from this man or his equivalent, for if this man is not the divine selection, you will not want him. As you are one with God, you are one with the love which belongs to you by divine right."

40

Several months passed, and matters remained about the same, but she was working conscientiously with herself. I said, "When you are no longer disturbed by his cruelty, he will cease to be cruel, as you are attracting it through your own emotions."

Then I told her of a brotherhood in India, who never said, "Good Morning" to each other. They used these words: "I salute the Divinity in you." They saluted the divinity in every man, and in the wild animals in the jungle, and they were never harmed, for they saw only God in every living thing. I said, "Salute the divinity in this man, and say, 'I see your divine self only. I see you as God sees you, perfect, made in His image and likeness.'"

She found she was becoming more poised and gradually losing her resentment. He was a Captain, and she always called him "The Cap." One day, she said suddenly, "God bless the Cap wherever he is."

I replied: "Now that is real love, and when you have become a 'complete circle,' and are no longer disturbed by the situation, you will have his love, or attract its equivalent."

I was moving at this time, and did not have a telephone, so was out of touch with her for a few weeks, when one morning I received a letter saying, "We are married."

At the earliest opportunity, I paid her a call. My first words were, "What happened?"

"Oh," she exclaimed, "a miracle! One day I woke up and all suffering had ceased. I saw him that evening and he asked me to marry him. We were married in about a week, and I have never seen a more devoted man."

There is an old saying: "No man is your enemy, no man is your friend, every man is your teacher." So one should become impersonal and learn what each man has to teach him, and soon he would learn his lessons and be free. The woman's lover was teaching her selfless love, which every man, sooner or later, must learn.

Suffering is not necessary for man's development; it is the result of violation of spiritual law, but few people seem able to rouse themselves from their "soul sleep" without it. When people are happy, they usually become selfish, and automatically the law of Karma is set in action. Man often suffers loss through lack of appreciation.

I knew a woman who had a very nice husband, but she said often, "I don't care anything about being married, but that is nothing against my husband. I'm simply not interested in married life."

She had other interests, and scarcely remembered she had a husband. She only thought of him when she saw him. One day her husband told her he was in love with another woman, and left. She came to me in distress and resentment.

I replied, "It is exactly what you spoke the word for. You said you didn't care anything about being married, so the subconscious worked to get you unmarried."

She said, "Oh yes, I see. People get what they want, and then feel very much hurt."

She soon became in perfect harmony with the situation, and knew they were both much happier apart.

When a woman becomes indifferent or critical, and ceases to be an inspiration to her husband, he misses the stimulus of their early relationship and is restless and unhappy.

A man came to me dejected, miserable and poor. His wife was interested in the "Science of Numbers," and had had him read. It seems the report was not very favorable, for he said, "My wife says I'll never amount to anything because I am a two."

I replied, "I don't care what your number is, you are a perfect idea in divine mind, and we will demand the success and prosperity which are already planned for you by that Infinite Intelligence."

Within a few weeks, he had a very fine position, and a year or two later, he achieved a brilliant success as a writer. No man is a success in business unless he loves his work. The picture the artist paints for love (of his art) is his greatest work. No man can attract money if he despises it. Many people are kept in poverty by saying: "Money means nothing to me, and I have a contempt for people who have it." This is the reason so many artists are poor. Their contempt for money separates them from it. I remember hearing one artist say of another, "He's no good as an artist, he has money in the bank."

This attitude of mind, of course, separates man from his supply; he must be in harmony with a thing in order to attract it.

Money is God in manifestation as freedom from want and limitation, but it must be always kept in circulation and put to right uses. Hoarding and saving react with grim vengeance.

This does not mean that man should not have houses and lots, stocks and bonds. It means man should not hoard even the principal, if an occasion arises, when money is necessary. In letting it go out fearlessly and cheerfully he opens the way for more to come in, for God is man's unfailing and inexhaustible supply.

This is the spiritual attitude towards money and the great Bank of the Universal never fails!

We see an example of hoarding in the film production of "Greed." The woman won five thousand dollars in a lottery, but would not spend it. She hoarded and saved, let her husband suffer and starve, and eventually she scrubbed floors for a living. She loved the money itself and put it above everything, and one night she was murdered and the money taken from her.

This is an example of where "love of money is the root of all evil." Money in itself, is good and beneficial, but used for destructive purposes, hoarded and saved, or considered more important than love, brings disease and disaster, and the loss of the money itself.

Follow the path of love, and all things are added, for God is love, and God is supply; follow the path of selfishness and greed, and the supply vanishes, or man is separated from it.

For example: I knew the case of a very rich woman who hoarded her income. She rarely gave anything away, but bought and bought things for herself. She was very fond of necklaces, and a friend once asked her how many she possessed. She replied, "Sixty-seven." She bought

43

them and put them away, carefully wrapped in tissue paper. Had she used the necklaces it would have been quite legitimate, but she was violating "the law of use." Her closets were filled with clothes she never wore, and jewels which never saw the light.

The woman's arms were gradually becoming paralyzed from holding on to things, and eventually she was considered incapable of looking after her affairs and her wealth was handed over to others to manage.

So man, in ignorance of the law, brings about his own destruction.

All disease, all unhappiness, come from the violation of the law of love. Man's boomerangs of hate, resentment and criticism, come back laden with sickness and sorrow. Love seems almost a lost art, but the man with the knowledge of spiritual law knows it must be regained, for without it, he has "become as sounding brass and tinkling cymbals."

For example: I had a student who came to me, month after month, to clean her consciousness of resentment. After a while, she arrived at the point where she resented only one woman, but that one woman kept her busy. Little by little she became poised and harmonious, and one day, all resentment was wiped out.

She came in radiant, and exclaimed "You can't understand how I feel! The woman said something to me and instead of being furious I was loving and kind, and she apologized and was perfectly lovely to me. Noone can understand the marvelous lightness I feel within!"

Love and good-will are invaluable in business. For example: A woman came to me, complaining of her employer. She said she was cold and critical and knew she did not want her in the position.

"Well," I replied, "Salute the Divinity in the woman and send her love."

She said "I can't; she's a marble woman."

I answered, "You remember the story of the sculptor who asked for a certain piece of marble. He was asked why he wanted it, and he replied, 'because there is an angel in the marble,' and out it he produced a wonderful work of art."

She said, "Very well, I'll try it." A week later she came back and said,

"I did what you told me to, and now the woman is very kind, and took me out in her car."

People are sometimes filled with remorse for having done someone an unkindness, perhaps years ago. If the wrong cannot be righted, its effect can be neutralized by doing someone a kindness in the present.

Sorrow, regret and remorse tear down the cells of the body, and poison the atmosphere of the individual.

A woman said to me in deep sorrow, "Treat me to be happy and joyous, for my sorrow makes me so irritable with members of my family that I keep making more Karma."

I was asked to treat a woman who was mourning for her daughter. I denied all belief in loss and separation, and affirmed that God was the woman's joy, love and peace. The woman gained her poise at once, but sent word by her son not to treat any longer, because she was "so happy, it wasn't respectable."

So "mortal mind" loves to hang on to its griefs and regrets. I knew a woman who went about bragging of her troubles, so, of course, she always had something to brag about. The old idea was if a woman did not worry about her children, she was not a good mother. Now, we know that mother-fear is responsible for many of the diseases and accidents which come into the lives of children. For fear pictures vividly the disease or situation feared, and these pictures objectify, if not neutralized. Happy is the mother who can say sincerely that she puts her child in God's hands, and knows therefore, that he is divinely protected.

For example: A woman awoke suddenly in the night feeling her brother was in great danger. Instead of giving in to her fears, she commenced making statements of Truth, saying, "Man is a perfect idea in Divine Mind, and is always in his right place, therefore, my borther is in his right place, and is divinely protected." The next day she found that her brother had been in close proximity to an explosion in a mine, but had miraculously escaped.

So man is his brother's keeper (in thought) and every man should know that the thing he loves dwells in "the secret place of the most high, and abides under the shadow of the Almighty."

"There shall no evil befall thee, neither shall any plague come nigh thy dwelling."

"Perfect love casteth out fear. He that feareth is not made perfect in love," and "Love is the fulfilling of the Law."

Chapter 8 - Intuition or Guidance

There is nothing too great of accomplishment for the man who knows the power of his word and who follows his intuitive leads. By the word he starts in action unseen forces and can rebuild his body or remold his affairs. It is, therefore, of the utmost importance to choose the right words, and the student carefully selects the affirmation he wishes to catapult into the invisible. He knows that God is his supply, that there is a supply for every demand, and that his spoken word releases this supply.

"Ask and ye shall receive."

Man must make the first move. "Draw nigh to God and He will draw nigh to you."

I have often been asked just how to make a demonstration.

I reply: "Speak the word and then do not do anything until you get a definite lead." Demand the lead, saying, "Infinite spirit, reveal to me the way, let me know if there is anything for me to do."

The answer will come through intuition (or hunch); a chance remark from someone, or a passage in a book, etc., etc. The answers are sometimes quite startling in their exactness. For example: A woman desired a large sum of money. She spoke the words: "Infinite Spirit, open the way for my immediate supply, let all that is mine by divine right now reach me, in great avalanches of abundance." Then she added: "Give me a definite lead, let me know if there is anything for me to do."

The thought came quickly, "Give a certain friend" (who had helped her spiritually) "a hundred dollars." She told her friend, who said, "Wait and get another lead, before giving it." So she waited, and that day met a woman who said to her, "I gave someone a dollar today; it was just as much for me as it would be for you to give someone a hundred."

This was indeed an unmistakable lead, so she knew she was right in giving the hundred dollars. It was a gift which proved a great investment, for shortly after that, a large sum of money came to her in a remarkable way.

Giving opens the way for receiving. In order to create activity in finances, one should give. Tithing, or giving one-tenth of one's income, is an old Jewish custom, and is sure to bring increase. Many of the richest men in this country have been tithers, and I have never known it to fail as an investment.

The tenth-part goes forth and returns blessed and multiplied. But the gift or tithe must be given with love and cheerfulness, for "God loveth a cheerful giver." Bills should be paid cheerfully, all money should be sent forth fearlessly and with a blessing.

This attitude of mind makes man master of money. It is his to obey, and his spoken word then opens vast reservoirs of wealth. Man, himself, limits his supply by his limited vision. Sometimes the student has a great realization of wealth, but is afraid to act.

The vision and action must go hand in hand, as in the case of the man who bought the fur-lined overcoat.

A woman came to me asking me to "speak the word" for a position. So I demanded: "Infinite Spirit, open the way for this woman's right position." Never ask for just "a position"; ask for the right position, the place already planned in Divine Mind, as it is the only one that will give satisfaction.

I then gave thanks that she had already received, and that it would manifest quickly. Very soon, she had three positions offered her, two in New York and one in Palm Beach, and she did not know which to choose. I said, "Ask for a definite lead."

47

The time was almost up and was still undecided, when one day, she telephoned, "When I woke up this morning, I could smell Palm Beach." She had been there before and knew its balmy fragrance.

I replied: "Well, if you can smell Palm Beach from here, it is certainly your lead." She accepted the position, and it proved a great success. Often one's lead comes at an unexpected time.

One day, I was walking down the street, when I suddenly felt a strong urge to go to a certain bakery, a block or two away.

The reasoning mind resisted, arguing, "There is nothing there that you want."

However, I had learned not to reason, so I went to the bakery, looked at everything, and there was certainly nothing there that I wanted, but coming out I encountered a woman I had thought of often, and who was in great need of the help which I could give her. So often, one goes for one thing and finds another.

Intuition is a spiritual faculty and does not explain, but simply points the way.

A person often receives a lead during a "treatment." The idea that comes may seem quite irrelevant, but some of God's leadings are "mysterious."

In the class, one day, I was treating that each individual would receive a definite lead. A woman came to me afterwards, and said: "While you were treating, I got the hunch to take my furniture out of storage and get an apartment." The woman had come to be treated for health. I told her I knew in getting a home of her own her health would improve, and I added, "I believe your trouble, which is a congestion, has come from having things stored away. Congestion of things causes congestion in the body. You have violated the law of use, and your body is paying the penalty."

So I gave thanks that "Divine order was established in her mind, body and affairs."

People little dream of how their affairs react on the body. There is a

48

mental correspondence for every disease. A person might receive instantaneous healing through the realization of his body being a perfect idea in Divine Mind, and, therefore, whole and perfect, but if he continues his destructive thinking, hoarding, hating, fearing, condemning, the disease will return.

Many people have attracted disease and unhappiness through condemnation of others. What man condemns in others, he attracts to himself.

For example: A friend came to me in anger and distress because her husband had deserted her for another woman. She condemned the other woman, and said continually, "She knew he was a married man, and had no right to accept his attentions."

I replied: "Stop condemning the woman, bless her, and be through with the situation, otherwise you are attracting the same thing to yourself."

She was deaf to my words, and a year or two later, became deeply interested in a married man, herself.

Man picks up a live-wire whenever he criticises or condemns, and may expect a shock.

Indecision is a stumbling-block in many a pathway. In order to overcome it, make the statement repeatedly, "I am always under direct inspiration; I make right decisions, quickly." These words impress the subconscious, and soon one finds himself awake and alert, making his right moves without hesitation.

I have found it destructive to look to the psychic plane for guidance, as it is the plane of many minds and not the "The One Mind." As man opens his mind to subjectivity, he becomes a target for destructive forces. The psychic plane is the result of man's mortal thought, and is on the "plane of opposites." He may receive either good or bad messages.

The science of numbers and the reading of horoscopes keep man down on the mental (or mortal) plane, for they deal only with the Karmic path. I know of a man who should have been dead, years ago, according to his horoscope, but he is alive and a leader of one of the biggest movements in this country for the uplift of humanity.

It takes a very strong mind to neutralize a prophecy of evil. The student should declaire, "Every false prophecy shall come to naught; every plan my Father in heaven has not planned, shall be dissolved and dissipated, the divine idea now comes to pass."

However, if any good message has ever been given one, of coming happiness or wealth, harbor and expect it and it will manifest sooner or later, through the law of expectancy. Man's will should be used to back the universal will. "I will that the will of God be done." It is God's will to give every man, every righteous desire of his heart, and man's will should be used to hold the perfect vision, without wavering.

As man becomes spiritually awakened he reconizes that any external inharmony is the correspondence of mental inharmony. If he stumbles or falls, he may know he is stumbling or falling in consciousness.

One day, a student was walking along the street condemning someone in her thoughts. She was saying mentally, "That woman is the most disagreeable woman on earth," when suddenly three boy scouts rushed around the corner and almost knocked her over. She did not condemn the boy scouts, but immediately called on the law of forgiveness, and "saluted the divinity" in the woman. Wisdom's way are ways of pleasantness and all her paths are peace.

When one has made his demands upon the Universal, he must be ready for surprises. Everything may seem to be going wrong when in reality, it is going right.

For example: A woman was told that there was no loss in divine mind, therefore, she could not lose anything which belonged to her; anything lost would be returned, or she would receive its equivalent. Several years previously, she had lost two thousand dollars. She had loaned the money to a relative during her lifetime, but the relative had died, leaving no mention of it in her will. The woman was resentful and angry, and as she had no written statement of the transaction, she never received the money, so she determined to deny the loss and collect the two thousand dollars from the Bank of the Universal. She had to begin by forgiving the woman, as resentment and unforgiveness close the doors of this wonderful bank.

She made this statement, "I deny loss; there is no loss in Divine Mind, therefore, I cannot lose the two thousand dollars which belong to me by divine right. As one door shuts another door opens."

She was living in an apartment house which was for sale, and in the lease was a clause stating that if the house was sold, the tenants would be required to move out within ninety days. Suddenly, the landlord broke the leases and raised the rent. Again, injustice was on her pathway, but this time she was undisturbed. She blessed the landlord, and said, "As the rent has been raised, it means that I'll be that much richer, for God is my supply." New leases were made out for the advanced rent, but by some divine mistake, the ninety days clause had been forgotten.

Soon after, the landlord had an opportunity to sell the house. On account of the mistake in the new leases, the tenants held possession for another year. The agent offered each tenant two hundred dollars if he would vacate. Several families moved; three remained, including the woman. A month or two passed, and the agent again appeared. This time he said to the woman, "Will you break your lease for the sum of fifteen hundred dollars?" It flashed upon her, "Here comes the two thousand dollars." She remembered having said to friends in the house, "We will all act together if anything more is said about leaving." So her lead was to consult her friends.

These friends said, "Well, if they have offered you fifteen hundred they will certainly give two thousand." So she received a check for two thousand dollars for giving up the apartment. It was certainly a remarkable working of the law, and the apparent injustice was merely opening the way for her demonstration.

It proved that there is no loss, and when man takes his spiritual stand he collects all that is his from this great Reservoir of Good.

Chapter 9 - Perfect Self Expression or The Divine Design

There is for each man perfect self-expression. There is a place which he is to fill and no one else can fill, something which he is to do, which no one else can do; it is his destiny!

This achievement is held, a perfect idea in Divine Mind, awaiting man's recognition. As the imaging faculty is the creative faculty, it is necessary for man to see the idea before it can manifest.

So man's highest demand is for the Divine Design of his life. He may not have the faintest conception of what it is, for there is possibly some marvelous talent hidden deep within him. His demand should be: "Infinite Spirit, open the way for the Divine Design of my life to manifest; let the genius within me now be released; let me see clearly the perfect plan."

The perfect plan includes health, wealth, love and perfect self-expression. This is the square of life, which brings perfect happiness. When one has made this demand, he may find great changes taking place in his life, for nearly every man has wandered far from the Divine Design.

I know, in one woman's case, it was as though a cyclone had struck her affairs, but readjustments came quickly and new and wonderful conditions took the place of old ones.

Perfect self-expression will never be labor; but of such absorbing interest that it will seem almost like play. The student knows, also, as man comes into the world financed by God, the supply needed for his perfect self-expression will be at hand.

Many a genius has struggled for years with the problem of supply, when his spoken word, and faith, would have released quickly the necessary funds.

For example: After the class one day, a man came to me and handed me a cent. He said: "I have just seven cents in the world, and I'm going to give you one; for I have faith in the power of your spoken word. I want you to speak the word for my perfect self-expression and prosperity."

I "spoke the word," and did not see him again until a year later. He came in one day, successful and happy, with a roll of yellow bills in his pocket. He said, "Immediately after you spoke the word, I had a position offered me in a distant city, and am now demonstrating health, happiness and supply."

A woman's perfect self-expression may be in becoming a perfect wife, a perfect mother, a perfect homemaker and not necessarily in having a public career.

Demand definite leads, and the way will be made easy and successful.

One should not visualize or force a mental picture. When he demands the Divine Design to come into his conscious mind, he will receive flashes of inspiration, and begin to see himself making some great accomplishment. This is the picture, or idea, he must hold without wavering.

The thing man seeks is seeking him - the telephone was seeking Bell!

Parents should never force careers and professions upon their children. With a knowledge of spiritual Truth, the Divine Plan could be spoken for early in childhood, or prenatally.

A prenatal treatment should be: "Let the God in this child have perfect expression; let the Divine Design of his mind, body and affairs be made manifest throughout his life, throughout eternity."

God's will be done, not man's; God's pattern, not man's pattern, is the command we find running through all the scriptures, and the Bible is a book dealing with the science of the mind. It is a book telling man how to release his soul (or subconscious mind) from bondage.

The battles described are pictures of man waging war against mortal thoughts. "A man's foes shall be they of his own household." Every man is Jehoshaphat, and every man is David, who slays Goliath (mortal thinking) with the little white stone (faith).

So man must be careful that his is not the "wicked and slothful servant" who buried his talent. There is a terrible penalty to be paid for not using one's ability. Often fear stands between man and his perfect self-expression. Stage-fright has hampered many a genius. This may be overcome by the spoken word or treatment. The individual then loses all self-consciousness, and feels simply that he is a channel for Infinite Intelligence to express Itself through.

He is under direct inspiration, fearless, and confident; for he feels that it is the "Father within" him who does the work.

A young boy came often to my class with his mother. He asked me to "speak the word" for his coming examinations at school. I told him to make the statement: "I am one with Infinite Intelligence. I know everything I should know on this subject." He had an excellent knowledge of history, but was not sure of his arithmetic. I saw him afterwards, and he said: "I spoke the word for my arithmetic, and passed with the highest honors, but thought I could depend on myself for history and got a very poor mark." Man often receives a set-back when he is "too sure of himself," which means he is trusting to his personality and not the "Father within."

Another one of my students gave me an example of this. She took an extended trip abroad one summer, visiting many countries where she was ignorant of the languages. She was calling for guidance and protection every minute, and her affairs went smoothly and miraculously. Her luggage was never delayed nor lost! Accomodations were always ready for her at the best hotels and she had perfect service wherever she went. She returned to New York. knowing the language. She felt God was no longer necessary, so looked after her affairs in an ordinary manner.

Everything went wrong, her trunks delayed, amid inharmony and confusion. The student must form the habit of "practicing the Presence of God" every minute. "In all thy ways acknowledge him." Nothing is too small or too great.

Sometimes an insignificant incident may be the turning point in a man's life.

Robert Fulton, watching some boiling water simmering in a tea kettle saw a steamboat!

I have seen a student, often, keep back his demonstration through resistance or pointing the way. He pins his faith to one channel only, and dictates just the way he desires the manifestation to come, which brings things to a standstill.

"My way, not your way!" is the command of Infinite Intelligence. Like all Power, be it steam or electricity, it must have a non-resistant engine or instrument to work through, and man is that engine or instrument.

Over and over again, man is told to "stand still". "Oh Judah, fear not; but tomorrow go out against them, for the Lord will be with you. You shall not need to fight this battle; set yourselves, stand ye still, and see the salvation of the Lord with you."

We see this in the incidents of the two thousand dollars coming to the woman through the landlord when she became non-resistant and undisturbed, and the woman who won the man's love "after all suffering had ceased."

The student's goal is Poise! Poise is Power, for it gives God-Power a chance to rush through man, to "will and to do Its good pleasure."

Poised, he thinks clearly and makes "right decisions quickly." "He never misses a trick."

Anger blurs the visions, poisons the blood, is the root of many diseases, and causes wrong decision leading to failure.

It has been named one of the worst "sins," as its reaction is so harmful. The student learns that in metaphysics sin has a much broader meaning than in the old teaching. He finds that fear and worry are deadly sins. The are inverted faith, and through distorted mental pictures bring to pass the thing he fears. His work is to drive out these enemies (from the subconscious mind).

So as we read in the previous Chapters, man can only vanquish fear by walking up to the thing he is afraid of. When Jehoshaphat and his army prepared to meet the enemy, singing "Praise the Lord, for his mercy endureth forever," they found their enemies had destroyed each other and there was nothing to fight.

For example: A woman asked a friend to deliver a message to another friend. The woman feared to give the message, as the reasoning mind said, "Don't get mixed-up in this affair, don't give that message."

She was troubled in spirit for she had given her promise. At last, she determined to "walk up to the lion," and call on the law of divine protection. She met the friend to whom she was to deliver the message. She opened her mouth to speak it, when her friend said, "So and So has left town." This made it unnecessary to give the message, as the situation depended upon the person being in town. As she was willing to do it, she was not obliged to; as she did not fear, the situation vanished.

The student often delays his demonstration through a belief in incompletion. He should make this statement: "In Divine Mind there is only completion, therefore my demonstration is completed. My perfect work, my perfect home, my perfect health." Whatever he demands are perfect ideas registered in Divine Mind, and must manifest, "under grace in a perfect way." He gives thanks he has already received on the invisible, and makes active preparation for receiving on the visible.

One of my students was in need of a financial demonstration. She came to me and asked why it was not completed. I replied: "Perhaps you are in the habit of leaving things unfinished, and the subconscious has gotten into the habit of not completing (as the without, so the within)."

"I'll go home and finish something I commenced weeks ago, and I know it will be symbolic of my demonstration."

She sewed assiduously, and the article was soon completed. Shortly after, the money came in a most curious manner. Her husband was paid his salary twice that month. He told the people of their mistake, and they sent word to keep it.

When man asks, believing, he must receive, for God creates His own channels!

I have been sometimes asked, "Suppose one has several talents, how is he to know which one to choose?" Demand to be shown definitely. Say: "Infinite Spirit, give me a definite lead, reveal to me my perfect self-expression, show me which talent I am to make use of now."

I have known people to suddenly enter a new line of work, and be fully equipped with little or no training. So make the statement: "I am fully equipped for the Divine Plan of my life," and be fearless in grasping opportunities.

Some people are cheerful givers, but bad receivers. They refuse gifts through pride or some negative reason, thereby blocking their channels, and invariably find themselves eventually with little or nothing. For example: A woman who had given away a great deal of money had a gift offered her of several thousand dollars. She refused to take it, saying she did not need it. Shortly after that, her finances were "tied up", and she found herself in debt for that amount. Man should receive gracefully the bread returning to him upon the water - freely ye have given, freely ye shall receive.

There is always the perfect balance of giving and receiving, and though man should give without thinking of returns, he violates law if he does not accept the returns which come to him; for all gifts are from God, man being merely the channel.

A thought of lack should never be held over the giver.

For example: When the man gave the one cent, I did not say; "Poor man, he cannot afford to give me that." I saw him rich and prosperous, with his supply pouring in. It was this thought which brought it. If one has been a bad receiver, he must become a good one, and take even a postage stamp if it is given him, and open up his channels for receiving.

The Lord loveth a cheerful receiver, as well as a cheerful giver.

I have often been asked why one man is born rich and healthy, and another poor and sick.

Where there is an effect there is always a cause; there is no such thing as chance. This question is answered through the law of reincarnation. Man goes through many births and deaths, until he knows the truth which sets him free. He is drawn back to the earth plane through unsatisfied desire, to pay his Karmic debts, or to "fulfill his destiny."

The man born rich and healthy has had pictures in his subconscious mind, in his past life, of health and riches; and the poor and sick man, of disease and poverty. Man manifests, on any plane, the sum total of his subconscious beliefs.

Man's freedom comes through fulfilling his destiny, bringing into manifestation the Divine Design of his life.

Chapter 10 - Denials and Affirmations

"Thou shalt decree a thing, and it shall be established unto thee."

All the good that is to be made manifest in man's life is already an accomplished fact in divine mind and is released through man's recognition, or spoken word; so he must be careful to decree that only the Divine Idea be made manifest, for often he decrees, through his "idle words," failure or misfortune.

It is, therefore, of the utmost importance to word one's demands correctly, as stated in a previous Chapter. If one desires a home, friend, position or any other good thing, make the demand for the "divine selection."

For example: "Infinite Spirit, open the way for my right home, my right friend, my right position. I give thanks it now manifests under grace in a perfect way."

The latter part of the statement is most important. For example: I knew a woman who demanded a thousand dollars. Her daughter was injured and they received a thousand dollars indemnity, so it did not come in a "perfect way."

The demand should have been worded in this way: "Infinite Spirit, I give thanks that the one thousand dollars, which is mine by divine right, is now released, and reaches me under grace in a perfect way."

As one grows in a financial consciousness, he should demand that the enormous sums of money which are his by divine right, reach him under grace, in perfect ways. It is impossible for man to release more than he thinks is possible, for one is bound by the limited expectancies of the subconscious. He must enlarge his expectancies in order to receive in a larger way.

Man so often limits himself in his demands. For example: A student made the demand for six hundred dollars, by a certain date. He did receive it, but heard afterwards that he came very near receiving a thousand dollars, but he was given just six hundred, as the result of his spoken word.

Wealth is a matter of consciousness. The French have a legend giving an example of this. A poor man was walking along a road when he met a traveler, who stopped him and said: "My good friend, I see you are poor. Take this gold nugget, sell it, and you will be rich all your days."

The man was overjoyed at his good fortune and took the nugget home. He immediately found work and became so prosperous that he did not sell the nugget. Years passed, and he became a very rich man. One day he met a poor man on the road. He stopped him and said: "My good friend, I will give you this gold nugget, which, if you sell, will make you rich for life." The mendicant took the nugget, had it valued, and found it was only brass. So we see, the first man became rich through feeling rich, thinking the nugget was gold.

Every man has within himself a gold nugget; it is his consciousness of gold, of opulence, which brings riches into his life. In making his demands, man begins at his journey's end, that is he declares he has already received. "Before ye call I shall answer."

Continually affirming establishes the belief in the subconscious.

It would not be necessary to make an affirmation more than once if one had perfect faith! One should not plead or supplicate, but give thanks repeatedly, that he has received. "The desert shall rejoice and blossom as the rose." This rejoicing which is yet in the desert (state of consciousness) opens the way for release.

The Lord's Prayer is in the form of command and demand, "Give us this day our daily bread, and forgive us our debts as we forgive our debtors," and ends in praise, "For thine is the Kingdom and the Power and the Glory, forever. Amen." "Concerning the works of my hands, command ye me." So prayer is command and demand, praise and thanksgiving. The student's work is in making himself believe that "with God all things are possible."

This is easy enough to state in the abstract, but a little more difficult when confronted with a problem. For example: It was necessary for a woman to demonstrate a large sum of money within a stated time. She knew she must do something to get a realization (for realization is manifestation), and she demanded a "lead." She was walking through a department store when she saw a very beautiful pink enamel papercutter. She felt the "pull" towards it. The thought came. "I haven't a paper cutter good enough to open letters containing large cheques."

So she bought the papercutter, which the reasoning mind would have called an extravagance. When she held it in her hand, she had a flash of a picture of herself opening an envelope containing a large cheque, and in a few weeks, she received the money. The pink papercutter was her bridge of active faith.

Many stories are told of the power of the subconscious when directed in faith.

For example: A man was spending the night in a farmhouse. The windows of the room had been nailed down, and in the middle of the night he felt suffocated and made his way in the dark to the window. He could not open it, so he smashed the pane with his fist, drew in draughts of fine fresh air, and had a wonderful night's sleep.

The next morning, he found he had smashed the glass of a bookcase and the window had remained closed during the whole night. He had supplied himself with oxygen, simply by his thought of oxygen.

When a student starts out to demonstrate, he should never turn back. "Let not that man who wavers think that he shall receive anything of the Lord."

A colored student once made this wonderful statement, "When I asks the Father for anything, I puts my foot down, and I says: Father, I'll take nothing less than I've asked for, but more!" So man should never compromise: "Having done all - Stand." This is sometimes the most difficult time of demonstrating. The temptation comes to give up, to turn back, to compromise.

"He also serves who only stands and waits."

Demonstrations often come at the eleventh hour because man then lets go, that is, stops reasoning, and Infinite Intelligence has a chance to work.

For example: A woman asked me why it was she was constantly losing or breaking her glasses. We found she often said to herself and others with vexation, "I wish I could get rid of my glasses." So her impatient desire was violently fulfilled. What she should have demanded was perfect eyesight, but what she registered in the subconscious was simply the impatient desire to be rid of her glasses; so they were continually being broken or lost.

Two attitudes of mind cause loss: depreciation, as in the case of the woman who did not appreciate her husband, or fear of loss, which makes a picture of loss in the subconscious.

When a student is able to let go of his problem (cast his burden) he will have instantaneous manifestation.

For example: A woman was out during a very stormy day and her umbrella was blown inside-out. She was about to make a call on some people whom she had never met and she did not wish to make her first appearance with a dilapidated umbrella. She could not throw it away, as it did not belong to her. So in desperation, she exclaimed: "Oh God, you take charge of this umbrella, I don't know what to do."

A moment later, a voice behind her said: "Lady, do you want your umbrella mended?" There stood an umbrella mender.

She replied, "Indeed, I do."

The man mended the umbrella, while she went into the house to pay her call, and when she returned, she had a good umbrella. So there is always an umbrella mender at hand, on man's pathway, when one puts the umbrella (or situation) in God's Hands.

One should always follow a denial with an affirmation.

For example: I was called on the phone late one night to treat a man whom I had never seen. He was apparently very ill. I made the statement: "I deny this appearance of disease. It is unreal, therefore cannot register in his consciousness; this man is a perfect idea in Divine Mind, pure substance expressing perfection."

There is no time or space, in Divine Mind, therefore the word reaches instantly its destination and does not "return void." I have treated patients in Europe and have found that the result was instantaneous.

I am asked so often the difference between visualizing and visioning. Visualizing is a mental process governed by the reasoning or conscious mind; visioning is a spiritual process, governed by intuition, or the superconscious mind. The student should train his mind to receive these flashes of inspiration, and work out the "divine pictures," through definite leads. When a man can say, "I desire only that which God desires for me," his new set of blueprints is given him by the Master Architect, the God within. God's plan for each man transcends the limitation of the reasoning mind, and is always the square of life, containing health, wealth, love and perfect self-expression. Many a man is building for himself in imagination a bungalow when he should be building a palace.

If a student tries to force a demonstration (through the reasoning mind) he brings it to a standstill. He should act only through intuition, or definite leads. "Rest in the Lord and wait patiently. Trust also in him, and he will bring it to pass."

I have seen the law work in the most astonishing manner. For example: A student stated that it was necessary for her to have a hundred dollars for the following day. It was a debt of vital importance which had to be met. I "spoke the word," declaring Spirit was "never too late" and that the supply was at hand.

That evening she phoned me of the miracle. She said that the thought came to her to go to her safe-deposit box at the bank to examine some papers. She looked over the papers, and at the bottom of the box was a new one hundred dollar bill. She was astounded and said she knew she had never put it there, for she had gone through the papers many times.

Man should make an art of thinking. The Master Thinker is an artist and is careful to paint only the divine designs upon the canvas of his mind; and he paints these pictures with masterly strokes of power and decision, having perfect faith that there is no power to mar their perfection and that they shall manifest in his life the ideal made real.

All power is given man (through right thinking) to bring his heaven upon his earth, and this is the goal of the "Game of Life."

The simple rules are fearless faith, non-resistance and love!

May each reader be now freed from that thing which has held him in bondage through the ages, standing between him and his own, and "know the Truth which makes him free" - free to fulfill his destiny, to bring into manifestation the "Divine Design of his life, Health, Wealth, Love and Perfect Self-Expression." "Be ye transformed by the renewing of your mind."

Denials and Affirmations

For Prosperity

God is my unfailing supply, and large sums of money come to me quickly, under grace, in perfect ways.

For Right Conditions

Every plan my Father in heaven has not planned shall be dissolved and dissipated, and the Divine Idea now comes to pass.

For Right Conditions

Only that which is true of God is true of me, for I and the Father are ONE.

For Faith

As I am one with God, I am one with my good, for God is both the Giver and the Gift. I cannot separate the Giver from the gift.

For Right Conditions

Divine Love now dissolves and dissipates every wrong condition in my mind, body and affairs. Divine Love is the most powerful chemical in the universe, and dissolves everything which is not of itself!

For Health

Divine Love floods my consciousness with health, and every cell in my body is filled with light.

For the Eyesight

My eyes are God's eyes, I see with the eyes of spirit. I see clearly the open way; there are no obstacles on my pathway. I see clearly the perfect plan.

For Guidance

I am divinely sensitive to my intuitive leads, and give instant obedience to Thy will.

For the Hearing

My ears are God's ears, I hear with the ears of spirit. I am non-resistant and am willing to be led. I hear glad tidings of great joy.

For Right Work

I have a perfect work
In a perfect way;
I give a perfect service
For perfect pay.

For Freedom from all Bondage

I cast this burden on the God within, and I go free!

Your Word is Your Wand

Chapter 1 - Your Word is Your Wand

Man's word is his wand filled with magic and power!

Man has power to change an unhappy condition by waving over it the wand of his word.

In the place of sorrow appears joy, in the place of sickness appears health, in the place of lack appears plenty.

For example: A woman came for a treatment for prosperity. She possessed just two dollars in the world.

I said: "We bless the two dollars and know that you have the magic purse of the Spirit; it can never be depleted; as money goes out, immediately money comes in, under grace in perfect ways. I see it always crammed, jammed with money: Yellow bills, green bills, pink checks, blue checks, white checks, gold, silver and currency. I see it bulging with abundance!"

She replied: "I feel my bag heavy with money," and was so filled with faith that she gave me one of her dollars as a love offering. I did not dare refuse it and see lack for her, as it was important that I hold the picture of plenty. Shortly aferwards she was made a gift of six thousand dollars. Fearless faith and the spoken word brought it to pass.

The affirmation of the magic purse is very powerful, as it brings a vivid picture to the mind. It is impossible not to see your purse or wallet filled with money when using the words, "crammed, jammed." The imaging faculty is the creative faculty and it is important to choose words which bring a flash of the fulfillment of the demand.

Never force a picture by visualizing. Let the Divine Idea flash into your conscious mind; then the student is working according to the Divine Design.

"Ye shall know the Truth and the Truth shall make you free."

This means that man must know the Truth of every situation which confronts him. There is no Truth in lack or limitation. He waves over it the wand of His Word and the wilderness rejoices and blossoms as the rose.

Fear, doubt, anxiety, anger, resentment pull down the cells of the body, shock the nervous system and are the causes of disease and disaster.

Happiness and health must be earned by absolute control of the emotional nature.

Power moves but is never moved. When man stands calm and serene, has a good appetite, feels contented and happy when appearances are against him, he has reached mastery. Then he has the power to "rebuke the winds and the waves," to control conditions.

His word is his wand and he transmutes apparent failure into success. He knows his universal supply is endless and immediate and all his needs manifest instantly on the external.

For example, a woman at sea awoke in the morning hearing the fog-horns blowing. A dense fog had settled on the ocean with no apparent signs of clearing. She immediately spoke the word: "There are no fogs in Divine Mind, so let the fog be lifted! I give thanks for the sun!

Soon the sun came out, for man has dominion over the elements - over all created things.

Every man has power to lift the fog in his life. It may be a fog of lack of money, love, happiness or health.

Give thanks for the sun!

Chapter 2 - Success

There are certain words or pictures which impress the subconscious mind.

For example: A man called asking me to speak the word for his right work. I gave him the statement: "Behold I have set before thee the open door of destiny and no man shall shut it!"

It didn't seem to make much impression, so I was inspired to add: "And no man shall shut it for it is nailed back!"

The man was electrified and went out walking on air. Within a few weeks he was called to a distant city to fill a wonderful position which came about in a miraculous way.

I give another example of a woman who fearlessly followed a "hunch."

She was working for a small salary when she read my book, The Game of Life and How to Play It. The thought came in a flash to start in business for herself and open a Tearoom and Candy Shop. The idea staggered her at first, but it persisted, so she boldly went forth and procured a shop and assistants.

She "spoke the word for supply," for she did not have money to back her enterprise. It came in miraculous ways, and the shop opened! From the first day it was filled with people, and now it is "crammed jammed"; they stand stand in line and wait.

One day, being a holiday, her assistants became gloomy and said they could not expect to do much business. My student, however, replied that God was her supply and every day was a good day. In the afternoon an old friend came in to see the shop and bought a two pound box of candy. He gave her a check and when she looked at it she found it was for a hundred dollars. So, it was indeed a good day! One hundred dollars for a box of candy!

She says every morning she enters the shop with wonder and gives thanks that she had the fearless faith that wins!

AFFIRMATIONS

The decks are now cleared for Divine Action and my own comes to me under grace in a magical way.

I now let go of worn-out conditions and worn-out things. Divine order is established in my mind, body and affairs. "Behold, I make all things new."

My seeming impossible good now comes to pass; the unexpected now happens!

The "four winds of success" now blow to me my own. From North,

South, East and West comes my endless good.

The God in me is risen, I now fulfill my destiny Endless good now comes to me in endless ways.

I clap my cymbals and rejoice, for God goes before me making clear, easy and successful my way!

I give thanks for my whirlwind succes. I sweep all before me for I work with the Spirit and follow the Divine Plan of my life.

My Spiritual Sporting blood is up! I am more than equal to this situation.

I am awake to my good, and gather in the harvest of endless opportunities.

I am harmonious, poised and magnetic. I now draw to myself my own. My power is God's power and is irresistible!

Divine Order is now established in my mind, body and affairs. I see clearly and act quickly and my greatest expectations come to pass in a miraculous way.

There is no competition on the spiritual plane. What is rightfuly mine is given me under grace.

I have within me an undiscovered country, which is revealed to me now, in the name of God.

Behold! I have set before thee the open door of Destiny and no man shall shut it, for it nailed back.

The tide of Destiny has turned and everything comes my way.

I banish the past and now live in the wonderful now, where happy surprises come to me each day.

There are no lost opportunities in Divine Mind; as one door shuts another door is opened.

I have a magical work in a magical way, I give magical service for magical pay.

The genius within me is now released. I now fulfill my destiny.

I make friends with hindrances and every obstacle becomes a stepping-stone. Everything in the Universe, visible and invisible, is working to bring to me my own.

I give thanks that the walls of Jericho fall down and all lack, limitation and failure are wiped out of my consciousness.

I am now on the royal road of Success, Happiness and Abundance, all the traffic goes my way.

I will not weary of well-doing, for when I least expect it I shall reap.

God goes before me and the battle is won! All enemy thoughts are wiped out. I am victorious.

There are no obstacles in Divine Mind, therefore, there is nothing to obstruct my good.

All obstacles now vanish from my pathway. Doors fly open, gates are lifted and I enter the Kingdom of fulfillment, under grace.

Rhythm, harmony and balance are now established in my mind, body and affairs.

New fields of Divine activity now open for me and these fields are white with harvest.

Man's will is powerless to interfere with God's will. God's will is now done in my mind, body and affairs.

God's plan for me is permanent and cannot be budged. I am true to my heavenly vision.

The Divine Plan of my life now takes shape in definite, concrete experiences leading to my heart's desire.

I now draw from the Universal Substance, with irresistible power and determination, that which is mine by Divine Right.

I do not resist this situation. I put it in the hands of Infinite Love and Wisdom. Let the Divine idea now come to pass.

69

My good now flows to me in a steady, unbroken, ever-increasing stream of success, happiness and abundance.

There are no lost opportunities in the Kingdom. As one door shuts another door opens.

There is nothing to fear for there is no power to hurt. I walk up to the lion on my pathway and find an angel in armor, and victory in the name of God.

I am in perfect harmony with the working of the law. I stand aside and let Infinite Intelligence make easy and successful my way.

The ground I am on is holy ground. The ground I am on is successful ground.

New fields of Divine Activity now open for me. Unexpected doors fly open, unexpected channels are free.

What God has done for others He can do for me and more!

I am as necessary to God as He is to me, for I am the channel to bring His plan to pass.

I do not limit God by seeing limitation in myself. With God and myself all things are possible.

Giving precedes receiving and my gifts to others precede God's gifts to me.

Every man is a golden link in the chain of my good.

My poise is built upon a rock; I see clearly and act quickly. God cannot fail, so I cannot fail. "The warrior within me" has already won.

Thy Kingdom come in me, Thy will be done in me and my affairs.

Chapter 3 - Prosperity

Man comes into the world financed by God, with all that he desires or requires already on his pathway.

This supply is released through faith and the Spoken Word.

"If thou canst believe, all things are possible."

For example: A woman came to me one day to tell me of her experience in using an affirmation she had read in my book, "The Game of Life and How to Play It."

She was without experience but desired a good position on the stage. She took the affirmation: "Infinite Spirit, open the way for my great abundance. I am an irresistible magnet for all that belongs to me by Divine Right."

She was given a very important part in a successful opera.

She said: "It was a miracle, due to the affirmation, which I repeated hundreds of times."

AFFIRMATIONS

I now draw from the abundance of the spheres my immediate and endless supply. All Channels are free! All Doors are open! I now release the gold-mine within me. I am linked with an endless golden stream of prosperity which comes to me under grace in perfect ways. Goodness and mercy shall follow me all the days of my life and I shall dwell in the house of abundance forever. My God is a God of plenty and I now receive all that I desire or require, and more.

All that is mine by Divine Right is now released and reaches me in great avalanches of abundance, under grace in miraculous ways.

My supply is endless, inexhaustible and immediate and comes to me under grace in perfect ways.

All channels are free and all doors fly open for my immediate and endless, Divinely Designed supply.

My ships come in over a calm sea, under grace in perfect ways.

I give thanks that the millions which are mine by Divine Right, now pour in and pile up under grace in perfect ways.

Unexpected doors fly open, unexpected channels are free, and endless avalanches of abundance are poured out upon me, under grace in perfect ways.

I spend money under direct inspiration wisely and fearlessly, knowing my supply is endless and immediate.

I am fearless in letting money go out, knowing God is my immediate and endless supply.

Chapter 4 - Happiness

In that wonderful moving picture, "The Thief of Bagdad," we were told in letters of light that happiness must be earned!

It is earned through perfect control of the emotional nature.

There can be no happiness where there is fear, apprehension or dread. With perfect faith in God comes a feeling of security and happiness. When man knows that there is an invincible power that protects him and all that he loves, and brings to him every righteous desire of the heart, he relaxes all nervous tension and is happy and satisfied.

He is undisturbed by adverse appearances, knowing that Infinite Intelligence is protecting his interests and utilizing every situation to bring his good to pass.

"I will make a way in the wilderness and rivers in a desert."

Uneasy lies the head that wears a frown. Anger, resentment, ill-will, jealousy and revenge rob man of his happiness and bring sickness, failure and poverty in their wake.

Resentment has ruined more homes than drink and killed more people than war.

For example: There was a woman who was healthy and happy and married to a man she loved.

The man died and left part of his estate to a relative. The woman was filled with resentment. She lost weight, was unable to do her work, developed gallstones and became very ill.

A metaphysician called upon her one day. He said: "Woman, see what hate and resentment have done to you; they have caused hard stones to form in your body and only forgiveness and good-will can cure you."

The woman saw the Truth of the statement. She became harmonious and forgiving and regained her splendid health.

AFFIRMATIONS

I am now deluged with the happiness that was planned for me in the Beginning. My barns are full, my cup flows over with joy.

My endless good now comes to me in endless ways.

I have a wonderful joy in a wonderful way, and my wonderful joy has come to stay.

Happy surprises come to me each day. "I look with wonder at that which is before me."

I walk boldly up to the lion on my pathway and find it is a friendly airedale.

I am harmonious, happy, radiant; detached from the tyranny of fear.

My happiness is built upon a rock. It is mine now and for all eternity.

My good now flows to me in a steady unbroken, ever-increasing stream of happiness.

My happiness is God's affair, therefore, no one can interfere.

As I am one with God I am now one with my heart's desire.

I give thanks for my permanent happiness, my permanent health, my permanent wealth, my permanent love.

I am harmonious, happy and Divinely magnetic, and now draw to me my ships over a calm sea.

God's ideas for me are perfect and permanent.

My heart's desire is a perfect idea in Divine Mine, incorruptible and indestructible, and now comes to pass, under grace in a magical way.

Chapter 5 - Love

With love usually comes terrific fear. Nearly every woman comes into the world with a mythical woman in the back of her mind who is to rob her of her love.

She has been called "the other woman." Of course it comes from woman's belief in duality. So long as she visualizes interference, it will come.

It is usually very difficult for a woman to see herself loved by the man she loves, so these affirmations are to impress the truth of the situation upon her subconscious mind, for in reality there is only oneness.

AFFIRMATIONS

As I am one with God, the Undivided One, I am one with my undivided love and undivided happiness.

The light of the God within now wipes out all fear, doubt, anger and resentment. God's love pours through me, an irresistible magnetic current. I see only perfection and draw to me my own.

Divine Love, through me, now dissolves all seeming obstacles and makes clear, easy and successful my way. I love everyone and everyone loves me. My apparent enemy becomes my friend, a golden link in the chain of my good.

I am at peace with myself and with the whole world. I love everyone and everyone loves me.

The flood gates of my good now open.

Chapter 6 - Marriage

Unless marriage is built upon the rock of oneness it cannot stand; "Two Souls with but a single thought, two hearts that beat as one."

The poet understood this, for unless man and wife are living the same thoughts (or living in the same thought world), they must inevitably drift apart.

Thought is a tremendous vibratory force and man is drawn to his thought creations.

For example: A man and woman married and were apparently happy. The man became successful and his tastes improved, but the wife still lived in a limited consciousness.Whenever the man bought anything he went to the best shops and selected what he needed regardless of price. Whenever the wife went out she haunted the Five and Ten Cent Stores.

He was living (in thought), on Fifth Avenue and her thought world was on Third Avenue.

Eventually the break and separation came.

We see this so often in the cases of rich and successful men who desert their faithful, hardworking wives later in life. The wife must keep pace with her husband's taste and ambitions and live in his thought world, for where a man thinketh in his heart there is he.

There is for each person his "other half" or divine selection. These two are one in their thought worlds. These are the two "whom God has joined together and no man shall (or can) part asunder." "The twain shall be made one," for in the superconscious mind of each is the same Divine Plan.

AFFIRMATIONS

I give thanks that the marriage made in heaven is now made manifest upon earth. "The twain shall be made one" now and for all eternity.

Chapter 7 - Forgiveness

AFFIRMATIONS

I forgive everyone and everyone forgives me. The gates swing open for my good.

I call on the law of forgiveness. I am free from mistakes and the consequences of mistakes. I am under grace and not under karmic law.

Though my mistakes be as scarlet, I shall be washed whiter than snow.

What didn't happen in the Kingdom never happened anywhere.

Chapter 8 - Words of Wisdom

AFFIRMATIONS

Faith without nerve is dead.

There is never a slip 'twixt the right cup and right lip.

Never look or you'd never leap.

God works in unexpected places, through unexpected people, at unexpected times, His wonders to perform.

Power moves but is never moved.

Loving your neighbor means not to limit your neighbor in word, thought or deed.

Never argue with a hunch.

Christopher Columbus followed a hunch.

The Kingdom of Heaven is the realm of perfect ideas.

It is dark before the dawn but the dawn never fails. Trust in the dawn.

When in doubt play trumps; do the fearless thing.

Never do today what intuition says to do tomorrow.

It's a great life if you don't reason.

Regard your neighbor as yourself.

Never hinder another's hunch.

Selfishness binds and blocks. Every loving and unselfish thought has in it the germ of success.

Be not weary of make-believing. When you least expect it you shall reap.

Faith is elastic. Stretch it to the end of your demonstration.

Before you call you are answered, for the supply precedes the demand.

What you do for others you are doing for yourself.

Every act committed while angry or resentful brings unhappy reaction.

Sorrow and disappointment follow in the wake of deceit and subterfuge. The way of the transgressor is hard.

No good thing will be withheld from him who walks uprightly.

There is no power in evil. It is nothing, therefore it can only come to nothing.

Fear and impatience demagnetize. Poise magnetizes.

Drown the reasoning mind with your affirmation. Jehoshaphat clapped his cymbals so that he wouldn't hear himself think.

All bonding is an illusion of the race consciousness. There is always a way out of every situation, under grace.

Every man is free to do the will of God.

Sure-ism is stronger than Optimism.

Divine ideas never conflict.

It is dangerous to stop in the middle of a hunch. Infinite Spirit is never too late.

Chapter 9 - Faith

Hope looks forward; Faith knows it has already received and acts accordingly.

In my classes I often emphasize the importance of digging ditches (or preparing for the thing asked for) which shows active faith and brings the demonstration to pass.

A man in my class, whom I called "the life of the party" because he always tried to find a question I couldn't answer, but he never succeeded, asked: "Why is it then, a lot of women who prepare Hope Chests never get married?" I replied: "Because it is a Hope Chest and not a Faith Chest."

The prospective bride also violates law in telling others about it. Her friends come in and sit on the Hope Chest and either doubt or hope she'll never succeed.

The student should never talk of a demonstration until it "has jelled," or comes to pass on the external.

So a Hope Chest should become a Faith Chest and be kept from the public eye, and the word spoken for the Divine Selection of a husband, under grace in a perfect way.

Those whom God hath joined together no thought can put asunder.

AFFIRMATIONS

Adverse appearances work for my good, for God utilizes every person and every situation to bring to me my heart's desire. "Hindrances are friendly" and obstacles are springboards! I now jump into my good!

As I am one with the Undivided One, I am one with my undivided good.

As the needle in the compass is true to the north, what is rightfully mine is true to me. I am the North!

I am now linked by an invisible, unbreakable magnetic cord with all that belongs to me by Divine Right!

Thy Kingdom is come, Thy will is done in me and my affairs.

Every plan my Father in heaven has not planned is dissolved and obliterated, and the Divine Design of my life now comes to pass.

What God has given me can never be taken from me for His gifts are for all eternity.

My faith is built upon a rock and my heart's desire now comes to pass, under grace in a miraculous way.

I see my good in a golden glow of glory. I see my fields shining white with the harvest.

I am poised and powerful; my greatest expectations are realized in a miraculous way.

I water my wilderness with faith and suddenly it blossoms as the rose.

God is my unfailing and immediate supply of all good.

I now exercise my fearless faith in three ways — by thinking, speaking and acting.

I am unmoved by appearances, therefore appearances move.

I stand steadfast, immovable, giving thanks for my seeming impossible good to come to pass, for I know, with God, it is easy of accomplishment, and His time is now.

God's plans for me are built upon a rock. What was mine in the beginning, is mine now and ever shall be mine.

I know there is nothing to defeat God, therefore, there is nothing to defeat me.

I wait patiently on the Lord, I trust in Him, I fret not myself because of evil doers (for every man is a golden link in the chain of my good) and He now gives to me the desires of my heart! (See 37th Psalm.)

I am in perfect harmony with the working of the law, for I know that

Infinite Intelligence knows nothing of obstacles, time or space. It knows only completion.

I give thanks that I now receive the righteous desires of my heart. Mountains are removed, valleys exalted and every crooked place made straight. I am in the Kingdom of fulfillment.

Before I called I was answered and I now gather in my harvest in a remarkable way.

I have now the fearless faith of the God within. At my approach barriers vanish and obstacles disappear.

I am steadfast, immovable, for the fields are already white with the harvest. My fearless faith in God now brings the Divine Design of my life to pass.

All fear is now banished in the name of God, for I know there is no power to hurt. God is the one and only power.

I now dig my ditches deep with faith and understanding and my heart's desire comes to pass in a surprising way.

My ditches will be filled at the right time, bringing all that I have asked for, and more!

I now "put to flight the army of the aliens" (negative thoughts); they feed on fear and starve on faith.

I am in perfect harmony with the working of the law, for I know that Infinite Intelligence knows nothing of obstacles, time or space. It knows only completion.

God works in unexpected and magic ways His wonders to perform.

I now prepare for the fulfillment of my heart's desire. I show God I believe His promise will be kept.

God's ideas cannot be moved, therefore, what's mine by Divine Right will always be with me.

I give thanks that I now receive the righteous desires of my heart.

I am in the Kingdom of fulfillment.

I have perfect confidence in God and God has perfect confidence in me.

God's promises are built upon a rock. As I have asked I must receive.

Let me never wander from my heart's desire.

I do not limit the Holy One of Israel, in word, thought or deed.

With God all things are easy and possible now.

I now stand aside and watch God work. It interests me to see how quickly and easily He brings the desires of my heart to pass.

He who watches over my heart's desire "Neither slumbers nor sleeps."

Seeming impossible doors now open, seeming impossible channels are free, in the name of God.

My good is a perfect and permanent idea in Divine Mind, and must manifest for there is nothing to prevent.

I cast every burden on God within and I go free!

Chapter 10 - Loss

If man loses anything, it shows there is a belief of loss in his subconscious mind. As he erases this false belief, the article or its equivalent will appear on the external.

For example: A woman lost a silver pencil in a theatre. She made every effort to find it but it was not returned.

She denied loss, taking the affirmation: "I deny loss, there is no loss in Divine Mind therefore I cannot lose that pencil. I will receive it or its equivalent."

Several weeks elapsed. One day she was with a friend who wore about her neck on a cord, a beautiful gold pencil, who turned to her and said: "Do you want this pencil? I paid fifty dollars for it at Tiffany's."

The woman was aghast, and replied (almost forgetting to thank her friend) "Oh! God aren't you wonderful! The silver pencil wasn't good enough for me!"

Man can only lose what doesn't belong to him by Divine Right, or isn't good enough for him.

AFFIRMATIONS

There is no loss in Divine Mind, therefore, I cannot lose anything that is rightfully mine.

Infinite Intelligence is never too late! Infinite Intelligence knows the way of recovery.

There is no loss in Divine Mind, therefore, I cannot lose anything that is rightfully mine. It will be restored or I will receive its equivalent.

Chapter 11 - Debt

If a man is in debt or people owe him money, it shows that a belief of debt is in his subconscious mind.

This belief must be neutralized in order to change conditions.

For example: A woman came to me saying a man had owed her a thousand dollars for years which she could not compel him to pay.

I said: "You must work on yourself, not the man," and gave her this statement: "I deny debt, there is no debt in Divine Mind, no man owes me anything, all is squared. I send that man love and forgiveness." In a few weeks she received a letter from him saying he intended to send the money and in about a month came the thousand dollars.

If a student owes money, change the statement: "There is no debt in Divine Mind, therefore, I owe no man anything, all is squared. All of my obligations are now wiped out, under grace in a perfect way."

AFFIRMATIONS

I deny debt, there is no debt in Divine Mind, therefore, I owe no man anything. All obligations are now wiped out under grace in a miraculous way.

I deny debt, there is no debt in Divine Mind, no man owes me anything, all is squared. I send forth love and forgiveness.

Chapter 12 - Sales

A woman who lived in a country town wished to sell her house and furniture. It was in the winter with snow so deep it was almost impossible for cars or wagons to reach her door. As she had asked God to sell her furniture to the right person for the right price she was unmindful of appearances.

She polished the furniture, pushed it into the middle of the room and prepared to sell it.

She said: "I never looked out of the window at the blizzard, I simply trusted God's promises." In miraculous ways people drove up and all the furniture was sold, and the house also, without paying any commission to an agent.

Faith never looks out of the window at the blizzard, it simply prepares for the blessing asked for.

AFFIRMATIONS

I give thanks that this article (or property) is now sold to the right person or persons for the right price, giving perfect satisfaction.

Chapter 13 - Interviews

AFFIRMATIONS

There is no competition on the Spiritual plane. What is mine is given me, under grace.

I am identified in love with the Spirit of this person (or persons). God protects my interest and the Divine Idea now comes out of this situation.

Chapter 14 - Guidance

Always on man's pathway is his message or his lead.

For example: A woman was much troubled over an unhappy situation. She thought to herself, "Will it ever clear up?"

Her maid was standing near and commenced to tell her of her experiences. The woman was too worried to be interested but listened patiently. The maid was saying: "I worked in a hotel once where there was a very amusing gardener, he always said such funny things. It had been raining for three days and I said to him: 'Do you think it will ever clear up?' And he replied, 'My God, doesn't it always clear up?'"

The woman was amazed! It was the answer to her thoughts. She said reverently, "Yes, with my God it always clears up!" Soon after, her problem did clear up in an unexpected way.

AFFIRMATIONS

Infinite Spirit, give me wisdom to make the most of my opportunities. Never let me miss a trick.

I am always under direct inspiration. I know just what to do and give instant obedience to my intuitive leads.

My angel of destiny goes before me, keeping me in the Way.

All power is given unto me to be meek and lowly of heart. I am willing to come last, therefore, I come first.

I now place my personal will upon the altar. Your will, not my will; Your way not my way; Your time not my time - and in the twinkling of an eye it is done!

There are no mysteries in the Kingdom. Whatever I should know will now be revealed to me, under grace.

I am a perfect non-resistant instrument for God to work through, and His perfect plan for me now comes to pass in a magic way.

Chapter 15 - Protection

AFFIRMATIONS

I am surrounded by the White Light of God, through which nothing negative can penetrate.

I walk in the Light of God and my fear giants dwindle into nothingness. There is nothing to oppose my good.

Chapter 16 - Memory

AFFIRMATIONS

There is no loss of memory in Divine Mind, therefore, I recollect everything I should remember and I forget all that is not for my good.

Chapter 17 - The Divine Design

There is a Divine Design for each man!

Just as the perfect picture of the oak is in the acorn, the divine pattern of his life is in the superconscious mind of man.

In the Divine Design there is no limitation, only health, wealth, love and perfect self-expression. So on man's pathway there is always a Divine Selection. Each day he must live according to the Divine Plane or have unhappy reactions.

For example: A woman moved into a new apartment which she had almost furnished, when the thought came to her: "On that side of the room should stand a Chinese cabinet!

Not long after, she was walking by an antique shop. She glanced in and there stood a magnificent Chinese cabinet about eight feet high, elaborately carved.

She entered and asked the price. The salesman said it was worth a thousand dollars but the woman who owned it was willing to take less. The man added: "What will you offer for it?" The woman paused and the price "Two hundred dollars" came into her mind, so she answered: "Two hundred dollars." The man said he would let her know if the offer was satisfactory.

She did not want to cheat anyone or get anything which was not rightfully hers, so going home she said repeatedly: "If it's mine I can't lose it and if it isn't mine, I don't want it." It was a snowy day and she said she emphasized her words by kicking the snow from right to left, clearing a pathway to her apartment.

Several days elapsed when she was notified that the woman was willing to sell the cabinet for two hundred dollars.

There is a supply for every demand, from Chinese cabinets to millions of dollars.

"Before ye call I shall answer," but, unless it is the Divinely Selected cabinet or millions, they would never bring happiness.

86

"Except the Lord build the house, they labor in vain that build it." (Psalm 127:1)

AFFIRMATIONS

I let go of everything not divinely designed for me, and the perfect plan of my life now comes to pass. What is mine by Divine Right can never be taken from me. God's perfect plan for me is built upon a rock.

I follow the magic path of intuition and find myself in my Promised Land, under grace.

My mind, body and affairs are now molded according to the Divine Pattern within.

God is the only power and that power is within me. There is only one plan, God's plan, and that plan now comes to pass.

I give thanks that I now bring forth from the Universal Substance everything that satisfies all the righteous desires of my heart.

The divine Design of my life now comes to pass. I now fill the place that I can fill and no one else can fill. I now do the things which I can do and no one else can do.

I am fully equiped for the Divine Plan of my life; I am more than equal to the situation.

All doors now open for happy surprises and the Divine Plan of my life is speeded up under grace.

Chapter 18 - Health

When man is harmonious and happy he is healthy! All sickness comes from violation of Spiritual Law. Resentment, ill-will, hate, fear, etc., etc., tear down the cells of the body and poison the blood. Accidents, old age and death itself, come from holding wrong mental pictures.

When man sees himself as God sees him, he will become a radiant being, timeless, birthless and deathless, for "God made man in His likeness and His image."

AFFIRMATIONS

I deny fatigue, for there is nothing to tire me. I live in the Kingdom of eternal joy and absorbing interests. My body is "the body electric," timeless and tireless, birthless and deathless.

Time and space are obliterated! I live in the wonderful now, birthless and deathless! I am one the The One!

Thou in me art:

Eternal joy.
Eternal youth.
Eternal wealth.
Eternal health.
Eternal love,
Eternal life.
I am a Spiritual Being - my body is perfect, made in His likeness and image. The Light now streams through every cell. I give thanks for my radiant health.

EYES - AFFIRMATIONS

(Imperfect vision. Correspondences—Fear, suspicion, seeing obstacles. Watching for unhappy events to come to pass—living in the past or future—not living in the NOW.)

The Light of God now floods my eyeballs. I have the crystal clear vision of the Spirit. I see clearly and distinctly there are no obstacles on my pathway. I see clearly the fulfillment of my heart's desire.

I have the X-ray eye of the Spirit. I see through apparent obstacles. I see clearly the miracle come to pass.

I have the crystal clear vision of the Spirit, I see clearly the open road. There are no obstacles on my pathway. I now see miracles and wonders come to pass.

I give thanks for my perfect sight. I see God in every face, I see good in every situation.

I have the crystal clear vision of the Spirit. I look up and down and all around, for my good comes from North, South, East and West.

My eyes are God's eyes, perfect and flawless. The Light of God floods my eyeballs and streams on my pathway. I see clearly there are no lions on my way, only angels and endless blessings.

ANEMIA - AFFIRMATIONS

(Correspondence —Unfed Desires—lack of happiness.)

I am nourished by the Spirit within. Every cell in my body is filled with light. I give thanks for radiant health and endless happiness. (This statement may be used in the healing of any disease.)

EARS - AFFIRMATIONS

(Deafness—Correspondence—Strong personal will, stubbornness and a desire not to hear certain things.)

My ears are the ears of Spirit. The Light of God now streams through my ears dissolving all hardness or malformation.

I hear clearly the voice of intuition and give instant obedience.

I hear clearly glad tidings of great joy.

RHEUMATISM - AFFIRMATIONS

(Correspondence — Faultfinding, criticism, etc.)

The Light of God now floods my consciousness dissolving all acid thoughts.

I love everyone and everyone loves me.

I give thanks for my radiant health and happiness.

FALSE GROWTHS - AFFIRMATIONS

(Correspondence—Jealousy, hatred, resentment, fear, etc., etc.)

Every plant my Father in Heaven has not planted shall be rooted up. All false ideas in my consciousness are now obliterated. The Light of God streams through every cell and I give thanks for my radiant health and happiness now and forevermore.

HEART DISEASE - AFFIRMATIONS

(Correspondence—Fear, Anger, etc.)

My heart is a perfect idea in Divine Mind and is now in its right place, doing its right work.

It is a happy heart, a fearless heart and a loving heart.

The Light of God streams through every cell and I give thanks for my radiant health.

Chapter 19 - Animals

AFFIRMATIONS

(Dog: for example)

I deny any appearance of disorder. This dog is a perfect idea in Divine Mind and now expresses God's perfect Idea of a perfect dog.

Infinite Intelligence illumines and directs this animal. It is a perfect idea in Divine Mind and is always in its right place.

Chapter 20 - The Elements

Man is made in God's likeness and image (Imagination) and is given power and dominion over all created things. He has the power to "rebuke the winds and the waves," check floods or bring rain when it is needed.

There is a tribe of American Indians who live in the desert country and depend on the power of prayer only, to bring rain to water their crops. They have a rain dance, which is a form of prayer, but no chief is allowed to take part who has any fear.

They give exhibitions of courage before they are admitted to the ceremonies.

A woman, who was an eye-witness, told me that out of a blue sky came a deluge of rain, the sun still shining.

AFFIRMATIONS
Fire:
Fire is man's friend and is always in its right place doing its right work.
Drought:
There is no drought in Divine Mind. I give thanks for the right amount of rain to nourish these crops or garden.

I see clearly this gentle downpour and the manifestation is now.
Storms:
The God within now rebukes the winds and the waves and there comes

a great calm. I see clearly peace established on land and sea.

Chapter 21 - Journey

AFFIRMATION

I give thanks for the Divinely planned journey under Divinely planned conditions with the Divinely planned supply.

Chapter 22

Miscellaneous

The thing you dislike or hate will surely come upon you, for when man hates, he makes a vivid picture in the subconscious mind and it objectifies.

The only way to erase these pictures is through non-resistance.

For example: A woman was interested in a man who told her repeatedly of his charming women cousins. She was jealous and resentful and he passed out of her life.

Later on she met another man to whom she was much attracted. In the course of their conversation he mentioned some women cousins he was very fond of. She resented it, then laughed, for here were her old friends "the cousins" back again.

This time she tried non-resistance. She blessed all the cousins in the Universe and sent them good-will, for she knew if she didn't, every man she met would be stocked up with women relations.

It was successfull for she never heard cousins mentioned again. This is the reason so many people have unhappy experiences repeated in their lives.

I knew a woman who bragged of her troubles. She would go about saying to people, "I know what trouble is!" and then wait for their words of sympathy.

Of course, the more she mentioned her troubles, the more she had, for by her words she "was condemned."

She should have used her words to neutralize her troubles instead of to multiply them.

For example - had she said repeatedly: "I cast every burden upon the God within and I go free," and not voiced her sorrows, they would have faded from her life, for "by your words you are justified."

"I will give to thee the land that thou seest." Man is ever reaping on the external what he has sown in his thought world.

For example: A woman needed money and was walking along the street making the affirmation that God was her immediate supply. She looked down and at her feet was a two dollar bill, which she picked up. A man standing near (a watchman in a building) said to her: "Lady, did you pick up some money? I thought it was a piece of chewing-gum paper. A lot of people walked over it, but when you came it opened up like a leaf."

The others, thinking lack, had passed over it, but at her words of faith it unfurled.

So with the opportunities in life - one man sees, another passes by.

"Without the vision my people perish." Unless man has some objective, some Promised Land to look forward to, he begins to perish.

We see it so often in small country towns, in the men who sit around a stove all winter, who "Ain't got no ambition."

Within each one is an undiscovered country, a gold mine.

I knew a man in a country town called "Magnolia Charlie," because he always found the first magnolia in the spring. He was a shoemaker, but every afternoon left his work to go to the station to meet the four-fifteen train from a distant city. They were the only romances in his life, the first magnolia and the four-fifteen train.

He felt vaguely the call of the vision in the superconscious mind. No doubt, the Divine Design for him included travel and perhaps he was to become a genius in the plant world.

Through the spoken word the Devine Design may be released and each

93

one fulfill his destiny.

Affirmation: "I now see clearly the perfect plan of my life. Divine enthusiasm fires me and I now fulfill my Destiny."

"Faith without works (or action) is dead."

The student, in order to bring into manifestation the answer to his prayer, must show active faith.

For example: A woman came to me asking me to speak the word for the renting of a room. I gave her the statement: "I give thanks that the room is now rented to the right and perfect man for the right price, giving perfect satisfaction."

Several weeks elasped but the room had not been rented.

I asked: "Have you shown active faith? Have you followed every hunch in regard to the room?" She replied: "I had a hunch to get a lamp for the room, but I decided I couldn't afford it." I said: "You'll never rent the room until you get the lamp, for in buying the lamp you are acting your faith, impressing the subconscious mind with certainty."

I asked: "What is the price of the lamp?" She answered: "Four dollars." I exclaimed:

"Four dollars standing between you and the perfect man!"

She became so enthusiastic, she bought two lamps.

About a week elapsed and in walked the perfect man. He did not smoke and paid the rent in advance and fulfilled her ideal in every way.

Unless you become as a little child and dig your ditches you shall in no wise enter the Kingdom of manifestation.

The Spiritual attitude towards money is to know that God is Man's supply, and that he draws it from the abundance of the spheres, through his faith and spoken word. When man realizes this he loses all greed for money and is fearless in letting it go out. W ith his magic purse of the Spirit, his supply is endless and immediate, and he knows also that giving preceeds receiving.

94

For example: A woman came to me asking me to speak the word for five hundred dollars by the first of August. (It was then about the first of July.)

I knew her very well, and said: "The trouble with you is you don't give enough. You must open your channels of supply by giving."

She had accepted an invitation to visit a friend and did not want to go on account of the formality. She said, "Please treat me to be polite for three weeks, and I want to get away as soon as possible, and be sure to speak the word for the five hundred dollars."

She went to the friend's house, was unhappy and restless and tried continually to leave, but was always persuaded to stay longer. She remembered my advice, however, and gave the people about her presents. Whenever possible she made a gift. It was nearing the first of August and no signs of the five hundred dollars, and no way of escape from the visit. The last day of July she said: "Oh God! Maybe I haven't given enough!" So she tipped all the servants more than she had intended.

The first of August, her hostess said to her: "My dear, I want to make you a gift," and she handed her a check for five hundred dollars!

God works in unexpected ways his wonders to perform.

AFFIRMATIONS

God is incapable of separation or division; therefore, my good is incapable of separation or division. I am one with my undivided good.

All that is mine by Divine Right is now released and reaches me in a perfect way under Grace.

God's work is finished now and must manifest.

There is no there —there is only here.

Reveal to me the way, let me see clearly the blessing which Thou hast given me.

95

Let Thy blessed will be done in me this day.

Hunches are my hounds of Heaven —they lead me in the perfect way.

I serve only faith and my unlimited abundance is made manifest.

I am undisturbed by appearances. I trust in God — and He now brings to me the desires of my heart.

All things I seek are now seeking me.

Divine Activity is now operating in my mind, body and affairs, whether I see it or not.

My good now overtakes me in a surprising way.

The Divine Plan of my life cannot be tampered with. It is incorruptible and indestructible. It awaits only my recognition.

Since I am one with the Only Presence, I am one with my heart's desire.

I now have the single eye of the Spirit and see only completion.

I am a perfect idea in Divine Mind and I am always in my right place doing my right work at the right time for the right pay.

The Columbus in you will see you through.

I am an irresistible magnet for checks, bills and currency—for everything that belongs to me by Divine Right.

Great peace have I who love thy law of non-resistance and nothing shall offend me.

Thou in me art Inspiration, Revelation and Illumination.

Thou in me art completion. As I have asked I must receive.

The law of God is the law of increase and I give thanks for increase under grace in perfect ways.

I dwell in a sea of abundance. I see clearly my inexhaustible supply. I see clearly just what to do.

My "World of the Wondrous" now swings into manifestation and I enter my Promised Land under grace!

Nothing is too good to be true.

Nothing is too wonderful to happen.

Nothing is too good to last.

Conclusion

Choose the affirmation which appeals to you the most and wave it over the situation which confronts you.

It is your magic wand, for your word is God in action.

"It shall not return void but shall accomplish that whereunto it is sent." (Isaiah 55:11)

The Secret Door to Success

This book consists of a series of addresses given by Mrs. Shinn, teaching the individual to control conditions and release abundance through a knowledge of Spiritual Law.

Chapter 1 - The Secret Door to Success

"So the people shouted when the priests blew with the trumpets; and it came to pass, when the people heard the sound of the trumpet, and the people shouted with a great shout, that the wall fell down flat, so that the people went up into the city, every man straight before him, and they took the city."--Joshua 6:20

A successful man is always asked, "What is the secret of your success?"

People never ask a man who is a failure, "What is the secret of your failure?" It is quite easy to see and they are not interested.

People all want to know how to open the secret door to success. For each man there is success, but it seems to be behind a door or wall. In the Bible reading, we have heard the wonderful story of the falling of the walls of Jericho. Of course all biblical stories have a metaphysical interpretation.

We will talk now about your wall of Jericho: the wall separating you from success. Nearly everyone has built a wall around his own Jericho. This city you are not able to enter contains great treasures - your divinely designed success, your heart's desire!

What kind of wall have you built around your Jericho? Often, it is a wall of resentment. Resenting someone, or resenting a situation, shuts off your good. If you are a failure and resent the success of someone else, you are keeping away your own success.

I have given the following statement to neutralize envy and resentment: What God has done for others, He now does for me and more.

A woman was filled with envy because a friend had received a gift. She made this statement and an exact duplicate of the gift was given her, plus another present.

It was when the children of Israel shouted that the walls of Jericho fell down. When you make an affirmation of Truth, your wall of Jericho totters.

I gave the following statement to a woman: The walls of lack and delay now crumble away, and I enter my Promised Land, under grace. She had a vivid picture of stepping over a fallen wall, and received the demonstration of her good almost immediately.

It is the word of realization which brings about a change in your affairs; for words and thoughts are a form of radioactivity. Taking an interest in your work, enjoying what you are doing opens the secret door of success.

A number of years ago I went to California to speak at the different centers, by way of the Panama Canal, and on the boat I met a man named Jim Tully. For years he had been a tramp. He called himself The King of the Hoboes. He was ambitious and picked up an education. He had a vivid imagination and commenced writing stories about his experiences. He dramatized tramp life, he enjoyed what he was doing, and became a very successful author. I remember one book called "Outside Looking In." It was made into a motion picture.

He is now famous and prosperous and lives in Hollywood. What opened the secret door to success for Jim Tully?

Dramatizing his life, being interested in what he was doing, he made the most of being a tramp.

On the boat, we all sat at the captain's table, which gave us a chance to talk. Mrs. Grace Stone was also a passenger on the boat; she had written the "Bitter Tea of General Yen," and was going to Hollywood to have it made into a moving-picture; she had lived in China and was inspired to write the book.

That is the Secret of Success, to make what you are doing interesting to other people. Be interested yourself, and others will find you interesting. A good disposition, a smile, often opens the secret door; the Chinese say, "A man without a smiling face must not open a shop."

The success of a smile was brought out in a French moving-picture in which Chevalier took the lead; the picture was called, "With a Smile." One of the characters had become poor, dreary and almost a derelict; He said to Chevalier "What good has my honesty done me?" Chevalier replied, "Even honesty won't help you, without a smile." So the man changes on the spot, cheers up, and becomes very successful.

Living in the past, complaining of your misfortunes, builds a thick wall around your Jericho.

Talking too much about your affairs, scattering your forces, brings you up against a high wall. I knew a man of brains and ability who was a complete failure. He lived with his mother and aunt, and I found that every night when he went home to dinner, he told them all that had taken place during the day at the office; he discussed his hopes, his fears, and his failures.

I said to him, "You scatter your forces by talking about your affairs. Don't discuss your business with your family. Silence is golden!"

He took my lead. During dinner he refused to talk about business. His mother and aunt were in despair. They loved to hear all about everything, but his silence proved golden! Not long after, he was given a position at one hundred dollars a week, and in a few years he had a salary of three hundred dollars a week.

Success is not a secret, it is a System.

Many people are up against the wall of discouragement. Courage and endurance are part of the system. We read this in lives of all successful men and women.

I had an amusing experience which brought this to my notice. I went to a moving picture theatre to meet a friend. While waiting, I stood near a young boy, selling programs. He called to people passing, "Buy a complete program of the picture, containing photographs of the actors and a sketch of their lives."

Most people passed by without buying. To my great surprise, he suddenly turned to me, and said,"Say, this ain't no racket for a guy with ambition!"

Then he gave a discourse on success. He said, "Most people give up just before something big is coming to them. A successful man never gives up."

Of course I was interested and said, "I'll bring you a book the next time I come. It is called The Game of Life and How to Play It. You will agree with a lot of the ideas."

A week or two later I went back with the book. The girl at the ticket office said to him, "Let me read it, Eddie, while you are selling programs." The man who took tickets leaned over to see what it was about. "The Game of Life" always gets people's interests.

I returned to the theatre in about three weeks; Eddie had gone. He had expanded into a new job that he liked. His wall of Jericho had crumbled, he had refused to be discouraged.

Only twice is the word success mentioned in the Bible - both times in the Book of Joshua.

"Only be strong and very courageous to observe to do according to all the law which Moses, my servant, commanded thee: turn not from it to the right nor to the left, that thou mayest have good success whithersoever thou goest. This book of the law shall not depart from thy mouth, but thou shalt meditate therein day and night, that thou mayest observe to do all that is written therein, for then shalt thou make thy way prosperous and thou shalt have good success. Turn not to the right nor to the left."

The road to success is a straight and narrow path; it is a road of loving absorption, of undivided attention.

You attract the things you give a great deal of thought to. So if you give a great deal of thought to lack, you attract lack, if you give a great deal of thought to injustice, you attract more injustice.

Joshua said, "And it shall come to pass, that when they make a long blast with the ram's horn, and when ye hear the sound of the trumpet, all the people shall shout with a great shout: and the wall of the city shall fall down flat, and the people shall ascend up, every man straight before him."

The inner meaning of this story is the power of the word, your word which dissolves obstacles and removes barriers. When the people shouted the walls fell down. We find in folklore and fairy stories, which come down from legends founded on Truth, the same idea - a word opens a door or cleaves a rock.

We have it again in the Arabian Night's Story, "Ali Baba and The Forty Thieves." I saw it made into a moving picture. Ali Baba has a secret hiding place hidden somewhere behind rocks and mountains and the entrance may only be gained by speaking a secret word. It is: "Open Sesame!"

Ali Baba faces the mountain and cries, "Open Sesame!" and rocks slide apart. It is very inspiring, for it gives you the realization of how YOUR own rocks and barriers will part at the right word.

So let us take the statement - The walls of lack and delay now crumble away, and I enter my Promised Land, under grace.

Chapter 2 - Bricks Without Straw

"There shall no straw be given you, yet ye shall make bricks without straw." --Exodus 5:18

In the 5th Chapter of Exodus, we have a picture of every day life, when giving a metaphysical interpretation. The Children of Israel were in bondage to Pharaoh, the cruel taskmaster, ruler of Egypt. They were kept in slavery, making bricks, and were hated and despised. Moses had orders from the Lord to deliver h is people from bondage: "Moses and Aaron went in and told Pharaoh --Thus saith the Lord God of Israel, Let my people go, that they may hold a feast unto me in the wilderness."

He not only refused to let them go, but told them he would make their tasks even more difficult: they must make bricks without straw being provided for them.

"And the task-masters of the people went out, and their officers, and they spake to the people, saying, Thus saith Pharaoh, I will not give you straw."

"Go ye, get you straw where ye can find it: yet not ought of your work shall be diminished."

It was impossible to make bricks without straw. The Children of Israel were completely crushed by Pharaoh; they were beaten for not producing the bricks. Then came the message from God. "Go therefore now, and work; for there shall no straw be given you, yet shall ye deliver the tale (number) of bricks."

Working with Spiritual law they could make bricks without straw, which means to accomplish the seemingly impossible.

How often in life people are confronted with this situation. Agnes M. Lawson in her "Hints to Bible Students" says, "The Life in Egypt under foreign oppression is the symbol of man under the hard taskmasters of Destructive thinking, Pride, Fear, Resentment, Ill-will, etc. The deliverance under Moses is the freedom man gains from the taskmasters, as he learns the law of life, for we can never come under grace, except we first know the law. The law must be made known in order to be fulfilled."

In the 111th Psalm we read in the final verse, "The fear of the Lord (law) is the beginning of Wisdom: a good understanding have all they that do his commandments: his praise endureth forever."

Now if we read the word Lord (law) it will give us the key to the statement.

The fear of the law (Karmic law) is the beginning of wisdom (not the fear of the Lord). When we know the whatever we send out comes back, we begin to be afraid of our own boomerangs.

I read in a medical journal the following facts telling of the Boomerang this great Pharaoh received.

It would appear that flesh is indeed heir to a long and ancient line of ills, when, as was revealed by Lord Monyahan at a lecture at Leeds, that the Pharaoh of the oppression suffered from hardening of the heart in a literal sense. Lord Monyahan showed some remarkable photographic slides of results of surgical operations a thousand years B.C., and among these was a slide of the actual anatomical remains of the Pharaoh of the Oppression.

"The large vessel springing from the heart was in such a well-preserved state, as to enable sections of it to be made recently from the lantern slide. It was impossible to distinguish between the ancient and modern vessel. Both hearts had been attacked by Atheroma, a condition in which calcium salts are deposited in the walls of the vessel, making it rigid and inelastic."

Inadequate expanse to the stream of blood from the heart caused the vessel to give way; with this condition went the mental changes that occur with a rigid arterial system: A narrowness of outlook, restriction and dread of enterprise, a literal hardening of the heart.

So Pharaoh's hardness of heart, hardened his own heart.

This is as true today as it was several thousand years ago - we are all coming out of the Land of Egypt, out of the House of Bondage. Your doubts and fears keep you in slavery; you face a situation which seems hopeless. What can you do? It is a case of making bricks without straw.

But remember the words of God, "Go therefore now, and work; for there shall no straw be given you, yet shall ye deliver the tale (number) of bricks." You shall make bricks without straw. God makes a way where there is no way!

I was told the story of a woman who needed money for her rent. It was necessary to have it at once, but she knew of no channel, she exhausted every avenue. However, she was a Truth student, and kept making her affirmations. Her dog whined and wanted to go out, she put on his leash and walked down the street, in the acustomed direction. However, the dog pulled at his leash and wanted to go in another direction. She followed, and in the middle of the block, opposite an open park, she looked down, and picked up a roll of bills, which exactly covered rent. She looked for ads, but never found the owner. There were no houses near where she found it.

The reasoning mind, the intellect, takes the throne of Pharaoh in your consciousness. It says continually, "It can't be done. What's the use!"

We must drown out these dreary suggestions with a vital affirmation!

For example take this statement: "The unexpected happens, my seemingly impossible good now comes to pass."

This stops all argument from the army of the aliens (the reasoning mind.)."The unexpected happens!" That is an idea it cannot cope with.

"Thou hast made me wiser than mine enemies." Your enemy thoughts, your doubts, fears and apprehensions!

Think of the joy of really being free forever from the Pharaoh of the oppression. To have the idea of security, health, happiness and abundance established in the subconscious. It would mean a life free from all limitation!

It would be the Kingdom where all things are automatically added unto us. I say automatically added unto us, because all life is vibration; and when we vibrate to success, happiness and abundance, the things which symbolize these states of consciousness will attach themselves to us.

Feel rich and successful, and suddently you receive a large cheque or a beautiful gift.

I tell the story showing the working of this law. I went to a party where people played games, and whoever won, received a gift. The prize was a beautiful fan. Among those present was a very rich woman who had everything. Her name was Clara. The poorer and resentful ones got together and whispered: "We hope Clara doesn't get the fan." Of course Clara won the fan. She was carefree and vibrating to abundance. Envy and resentment short-circuit your good and keep away your fans.

If you should happen to be resentful and envious, take the statement: What God has done for others He now does for me and more! Then all the fans and things will come your way.

No man gives to himself but himself, and no man takes away from himself but himself. The "Game of Life" is a game of solitaire; as you change, all conditions will change. Now to go back to Pharaoh the oppressor; no one loves an oppressor.

I remember a friend I had many years ago, her name was Lettie. Her father had plenty of money and supplied her mother and herself with food and clothes, but no luxuries. We went to Art School together, and all the students would buy reproductions of the "Winged Victory," "Whister's Mother" or something to bring art into their homes.

My friend's father called all these things "plunder." He would say, "Don't bring home any plunder." So she lived a colorless life without a "Winged Victory" on her bureau or "Whistler's Mother" on the wall.

He would say often to my friend and her mother, "When I die, you'll both be well off."

One day someone said to Lettie, "When are you going abroad?" (all art students went abroad.) She replied, cheerfully, "Not 'till Papa dies."

So people always look forward to being free from lack and oppression.

Let us now free ourselves from the tyrants of negative thinking. We have been slaves to doubts, fears and apprehension and let us be delivered as Moses delivered the Children of Israel and come out of the Land of Egypt, out of the House of Bondage. Find the thought which is your great oppressor; find the "king-pin".

In the logging camps in the Spring, the logs are sent down the rivers in great numbers. Sometimes the logs become crossed and cause a jam. The men look for the log causing the jam (they call it the king-pin), straighten it, and the logs rush down the river again. Maybe your King-Pin is resentment. Resentment holds back your good. The more you resent, the more you will have to resent; you grow a resentment track in your brain, and your expression will be one of habitual resentment. You will be avoided and miss the golden opportunities which await you each day.

I remember a few years ago, the streets were filled with men selling apples. They got up early to get the good corners. I passed one several

107

times on Park Avenue. He had the most disagreeable expression I have ever seen. As people passed, he said, "Apples! Apples!" but no one stpped to buy.

I invested in an apple and said, "You'll never sell apples unless you change your expression."

He replied, "Well that guy over there took my corner."

I said, "Never mind about the corner, you can sell apples right here if you'll look pleasant."

He said, "O.K. lady," and I went on. The next day I saw him, his whole expression had changed. He was doing a big business selling apples with a smile.

So find your king-pin (you may have more than one); and your logs of success, happiness and abundance will go rushing down your river.

"Go therefore now and work, for there shall no straw be given you, yet ye shall make bricks without straw."

Chapter 3 - Be Wise

The Bible teaches that true prayer means preparation. Only those who have prepared for their good (by showing active faith) will bring the manifestation to pass.

We might paraphrase the scriptures and say: When ye pray believe ye have it. When ye pray ACT as if you have already received.

Armchair faith or rocking chair faith, will never move mountains. In the armchair, in the silence, or meditation, you are filled with the wonder of this Truth, and feel that your faith will never waver. You know that The Lord is your Shepherd, you shall never want. You feel that your God of Plenty will wipe out all burdens of debt or limitations. Then you leave your armchair and step out into the arena of Life. It is only what you do in the arena that counts.

I will you give you an illustration showing how the law works; for faith without action is dead.

A man, one of my students, had a great desire to go abroad. He took the statement: I give thanks for my divinely designed trip, divinely financed, under grace, in a perfect way. He had very little money, but knowing the law of preparation, he bought a trunk. It was a very gay and happy trunk with a big red band around its waist. Whenever he looked at it it gave him a realization of a trip.

One day he seemed to feel his room moving. He felt the motion of a ship. He went to the window to breathe the fresh air, and it smelt like the aroma of the docks. With his inner ear he heard the shriek of a seagull and the creaking of the gangplank. The trunk had commenced to work. It had put him in the vibration of his trip. Soon after that, a large sum of money came to him and he took the trip. He said afterwards that it was perfect in every detail.

In the arena of Life we must keep ourselves tuned-up to concert pitch.

Are we acting from motives of fear or faith? Watch your motives with all diligence, for out of them are the issues of life.

If your problem is a financial one (and it usually is) you must know how to wind yourself up financially, and keep wound up by always acting your faith. The material attitude towards money is to trust in your salary, your income and investments, which can shrink overnight.

The spiritual attitude toward money is to trust in God for your supply. To keep your possessions, always realize that they are God in manifestation. Then if one door shuts, another door immediately opens.

Never voice lack or limitation for "by your words your are condemned." You combine with what you notice, and if you are always noticing failure and hard times, you will combine with failure and hard times.

You must form the habit of living in the fourth dimension, "The World of the Wondrous." It is the world where you do not judge by appearances.

You have trained your inner eye to see through failure into success, to see through sickness into health, to see through limitation into plenty. I will give you the land which you though seeth.

The man who achieves success has the fixed idea of succes. If it is founded on a rock of truth and rightness it will stand. If not, it is built upon sand and washed into the sea, returning to its native nothingness.

Only divine ideas can endure. Evil destroys itself, for it is a cross current against universal order, and the way of the transgressor is hard.

The man received the trip because it was in his consciousness, as a reality. He believed that he had already received. With realization comes manifestation.

The law of preparation works both ways. If you prepare for what you fear or don't want, you begin to attract it. David said, "The thing I feared has come upon me." We hear people say, "I must put away money in case of illness." They are deliberately preparing to be ill. Or, "I'm saving for a rainy day." The rainy day is sure to come, at a most inconvenient time.

The divine idea for every man is plenty. Your barns should be full, and your cup should flow over, but we must learn to ask aright.

For example take this statement: I call on the law of accumulation. My supply comes from God, and now pours in and piles up, under grace. This statement does not give any picture of stint or saving or sickness. It gives a fourth dimentional feeling of abundance, leaving the channels to Infinite Intelligence.

Every day you must make a choice, will you be wise or foolish? Will you prepare for your good? Will you take the giant swing into faith or serve doubt and fear? Every day examine your consciousness and see just what your are preparing for. You are fearful of lack and hang on to every cent, thereby attracting more lack. Use what you have with wisdom and it opens the way for more to come to you.

In my book, "Your Word Is Your Wand," I tell about the Magic Purse. In the Arabian Nights they tell the story of a man who had a Magic Purse. As money went out, immediately money appeared in it again.

So I made the Statement: My supply comes from God - I have the magic purse of the spirit. It can never be depleted. As money goes out, immediately money comes in. It is always crammed, jammed with abundance, under grace, in perfect ways. This brings a vivid picture to mind: You are drawing on the bank of the imagination.

A woman who did not have much money was afraid to pay any bills and see her bank account dwindle. It came to her with great conviction: "I have the magic purse of the spirit. It can never be depleted. As money goes out, immediately money comes in." She fearlessly paid her bills, and several large cheques came to her that she did not expect.

"Watch and pray lest ye enter into the temptation" of preparing for something destructive instead of something constructive.

I knew a woman who told me she always kept a long crepe veil handy in case of funerals. I said to her, "You are a menace to your relatives, and are preparing to hurry them all off, so that you can wear the veil." She destroyed it.

Another woman who had no money decided to send her two daughters to college. Her husband scorned the idea and said, "Who will pay their tuition? I have no money for it." She replied, "I know some unforeseen good will come to us." She kept on preparing her daughters for college. Her husband laughed heartily and told all their friends that his wife was sending the girls to college on "some unforeseen good." A rich relative suddenly sent her a large sum of money. "Some unforeseen good" did arrive, for she had shown active faith. I asked what she had said to her husband when the cheque arrived. She replied, "Oh, I never antagonize George by telling him I am in the right."

So prepare for your "unforeseen good." Let every thought and every act express your unwavering faith. Every event in your life is a crystallized idea, something you have invited through either fear or faith. Something you have prepared for. So let us be wise and act in faith - and when we least expect it, we shall reap the fruits of our faith.

Chapter 4 - What Do You Expect?

Faith is expectancy. We might say, according to your expectancies be it done unto you; so what are you expecting? We hear people say: "We expect the worst to happen," or "The worst is yet to come." They are deliberately inviting the worst to come. We hear others say: "I expect a change for the better." They are inviting better conditions into their lives.

Change your expectancies and you change your conditions.

How can you change your expectancies when you have formed the habit of expecting loss, lack or failure? Begin to act as if you expected success, happiness and abundance; prepare for your good. Do something to show you expect it to come. Active faith alone, will impress the subconscious. If you have spoken the word for a home, prepare for it immediately, as if you hadn't a moment to lose. Collect little ornaments, tablecloths, etc., etc.!

I knew a woman who made the giant swing into faith by buying a large armchair - a chair meant businesss She bought a large and comfortable chair, for she was preparing for the right man. He came.

Someone will say, "Suppose you haven't money to buy ornaments or a chair?" Then look in shop windows and link with them in thought. Get in their vibration.

I sometimes hear people say; "I don't go into the shops because I can't afford to buy anything." That is just the reason why you should go into the shops. Begin to make friends with the things you desire or require.

I know a woman who wanted a ring. She went boldly to the ring department and tried on rings. It gave her such a realization of ownership that not long after, a friend made her a gift of a ring. "You combine with what you notice."

Keep on noticing beautiful things, and you make an invisible contact. Sooner or later these things are drawn into your life, unless you say, "Poor me, too good to be true."

"My soul, wait thou only upon God for my expectation is from Him." This is a most important statement from the 62nd Psalm.

The soul is the subconscious mind, and the psalmist was telling his subconscious to expect everything directly from the universal, not to depend upon doors and channels; "My expectations is from Him."

God cannot fail, for "His ways are ingenious, His methods are sure."

You can expect any seemingly impossible Good from God, if you do not limit the channels. Do not say how you want it done, or how it can't be done. "God is the Giver and the Gift and creates His own amazing channels."

Take the following statement: I cannot be separated from God the Giver, therefore, I cannot be separated from God the Gift. The gift is God in action.

Get the realization that every blessing is Good in action, and see God in every face and good in every situation. This makes you master of all conditions.

A woman came to me saying that there was no heat in the radiators in their apartment, and that her mother was suffering from the cold. She added, "The landlord has declared that we can't have heat until a certain date." I replied, "God is your landlord." She said, "That's all I want to know," and rushed out. That evening the heat was turned on without asking. It was because she realized that the landlord was God in manifestation. This is a wonderful age, for people are becoming Miracle Minded; it is in the air.

Quoting from an article which I found in the New York Journal and American by John Anderson, it corroborates what I have just said. The title of the article is "Theatre Goers Make Hits of Metaphysical Plays."

"If", said the cynical manager - who shall be called Brock Pemberton - with a slight accent of sarcasm in his voice, "the other night, on an intermission curbside talk, you fellows meaning the critics, know so much about what the New York public wants, why don't you tell me what to produce?"

"Why don't you tell me what sort of play the play-goers want to see?" "I would," I said, "But you wouldn't believe it."

"You're hedging," he said, "You don't know, and you're trying to cover up by pretending to know more than you're willing to say. You haven't any more idea than I have this minute what sort of plays generally succeed."

"I have," I said, "there is one sure-fire success; one theme that works and has always worked, whether it is competing with boy meets girl, mysteries, historical tragedies, etc. No play on the theme has ever completely failed if it had nay merit at all, and a lot of poor ones have been big hits."

"You're stalling again," said Mr. Pemberton, "What sort of plays are they?"

"Metaphysical," I said, fouling slightly with a big word and waiting quietly for the effect.

"Metaphysical," said Mr. Pemberton, "You mean metaphysical?"

I paused a moment and since Mr. Pemberton said nothing, went right on spouting such titles as "The Green Pastures," "The Star Wagon," "Father Malachy's Miracle!", etc. "Some of these," I added, "reached the public over the heads of the critics." But Mr. Pemberton had departed to ask, probably in every theatre in town, "Is there a metaphysician in the house?"

People are beginning to realize the power of their words and thoughts. They understand why "Faith is the substance of the thing hoped for, the evidence of things not seen." We see the law of expectancy working out through superstition. If you walk under a ladder and expect it to give you bad luck, it will give you bad luck. The ladder is quite innocent; bad luck came because you expected it.

We might say, expectancy is the substance of the things hoped for, or expectancy is the substance of the thing man fears. "The thing I expected has come upon me." Nothing is too good to be true, nothing is too wonderful to happen, nothing is too good to last, when you look to God for your good.

114

Now think of the blessings which seem so far off, and begin to expect them now, under grace, in an unexpected way; for God works in unexpected ways, His wonders to perform.

I was told that there are three thousand promises in the Bible. Let us now expect all these blessings to come to pass. Among them we are promised Riches and Honor, Eternal Youth and Eternal Life. We now know that all these things are scientifically possible.

I expect the unexpected, my glorious good now comes to pass.

Chapter 5 - The Long Arm of God

"The Eternal God is thy refuge, and underneath are the everlasting arms." --Deut. 33:27

In the Bible, the arm of God always symbolizes protection. The writers of the Bible knew the power of a symbol. It brings a picture which impresses the subconscious mind. They used the symbols of the rock, sheep, shepherds, vineyard, lamp, and hundreds of others. It would be interesting to know how many symbols are used in the Bible. The arm also symbolizes strength.

"The eternal God is thy refuge, and underneath are the everlasting arms, and he shall thrust out the enemy from before thee and shall say, Destroy them."

Who is the enemy "before thee?" The negative thought-forms which you have built up in your subconscious mind. A man's enemies are only those of his own household. The everlasting arms thrust out these enemy thoughts and destroy them.

Have you ever felt the relief of getting out some negative thought-form? Perhaps you have built up a thought-form of resentment, until you are always boiling with anger about something. You resent people you know, people you don't know, people in the past and people in the present, and you may be sure that the people in the future won't escape your wrath.

All the organs of the body are affected by resentment, for when you resent, you resent with every organ of the body. You pay the penalty with rheumatism, arthritis, neuritis, etc., for acid thoughts produce acid in the blood. All this trouble comes because you are fighting the battle, not leaving it to the long arm of God.

I have given the following statement to many of my students. "The long arm of God reaches out over people and conditions, controlling this situation and protecting my interests."

This brings a picture of a long arm symbolizing strength and protection. With the realization of the power of the long arm of God, you would no longer resist or resent. You would relax and let go. The enemy thoughts within you would be destroyed, therefore, the adverse conditions would disappear.

Spiritual development means the ability to stand still, or stand aside, and let Infinite Intelligence lift your burdens and fight your battles. When the burden of resentment is lifted, you experience a sense of relief! You have a kindly feeling for everyone, and all the organs of your body begin to function properly.

A clipping quoting Albert Edward Day, D.D. reads, "That loving our enemies is good for our spiritual health is widely known and accepted. But that negation and poisonous emotions destroy physical health, is a relatively new discovery. The problem of health is often an emotional one. Wrong emotions entertained and repeated are potent causes of illness. When the preacher talks about loving your enemies, the man on the street is apt to dismiss the idea as unendurable and pious. But the fact is, the preacher is telling you something which is one of the first laws of hygiene, as well as ethics. No man even for his body's sake can afford to indulge in hatred. It is like repeated doses of poison. When you are urged to get rid of fear, you are not listening to a moonstruck idealist; rather you are hearing counsel that is as significant for health as advice about diet."

We hear so much about a balanced diet, but without a balanced mind you can't digest what you eat, calories or no calories.

Non-resistance is an art. When acquired, The World is Yours! So many people are trying to force situations. Your lasting good will never comes through forcing personal will.

"Flee from the things which flee from thee, Seek nothing, fortune seeketh thee. Behold his shadow on the floor! Behold him standing at the door!"

I do not know the author of these lines.

Lovelock, the celebrated English athlete, was asked how to attain his speed and endurance in running. He replied, "Learn to relax." Let us attain this rest in action. He was most relaxed when running the fastest.

Your big opportunity and big success usually slide in when you least expect it. You have to let go long enough for the great law of attraction to operate. You never saw a worried and anxious magnet. It stands up straight and hasn't a care in the world, because it knows needles can't help jumping to it. The things we rightly desire come to pass when we have taken the clutch off.

I say in my correspondence course, Do not let your heart's desire become your heart's disease." You are completely demagnetized when you desire something too intensely. You worry, fear, and agonize. There is an occult law of indifference -"None of these things move me." Your ships come in over a don't care sea.

Many people in Truth antagonize friends, because they are too anxious for them to read the books and go to the lectures. The meet opposition.

A friend took my book, "The Game of Life and How to Play It" to her brother's house to read. The young men of the family refused to read it. No "nut stuff" for them. One of these young men drives a taxi cab. One night he drove a taxi which belonged to another man. In going over the car he found a book stuffed away somewhere. It was "The Game of Life and How to Play It". The next day he said to his aunt, "I found Mrs. Shinn's book in the taxi last night. I read it and it's great! There's a lot of good reading in it. Why doesn't she write another book?" God works in roundabout ways, his wonders to perform.

I meet unhappy people and a few grateful and contented people. A man said to me one day, "I have a great deal to be thankful for; I have good health, enough money and I'm still single!"

117

The eighty-ninth psalm is very interesting, for we find that two individuals take part, the man who sings the psalm (for all psalms are songs or poems), and Lord God of Hosts answers him. It is a song of praise and thanksgiving, extolling the strong arm of God.

"I will sing of the mercies of the Lord forever!"

"O Lord God of Hosts, who is a strong Lord like unto thee?"

"Thou hast a mighty arm, strong is thy hand, and high is thy right hand."

Then the Lord of Hosts replies:

"With whom my hand shall be established, mine arm also shall strengthen him."

"My mercy will I keep for him for evermore, and my covenant shall stand fast with him."

We only hear the words "for evermore" in the Bible and in fairytales. In the absolute, man is outside of time and space. His good is "from everlasting to everlasting." The fairytales came down from the old Persian legends which were founded upon Truth. Aladdin and His Wonderful Lamp is the out-picturing of the Word. Aladdin rubbed the lamp and all his desires came to pass. Your word is your lamp. Words and thoughts are a form of radioactivity and do not return void. A scientist has said that words are clothed in light. You are continually reaping the fruits of your words.

A friend in one of my meetings said that she had brought a man to my class who had been out of work for a year or more. I gave the statement: "Now is the appointed time. Today is the day of my amazing good fortune." It clicked in his consciousness. Soon after, he was given a position which paid him nine thousand dollars a year!

A woman told me that when I blessed the offering, I said that each offering would return a thousandfold. She had put a dollar in the collection. She said with great realization, "That dollar is blessed and returns a thousand dollars." She received a thousand dollars a short time afterwards, in a most unexpected way.

Why do some people demonstrate this Truth so much more quickly than others? It is because they have the ears that hear. I say, "Listen for the statement that clicks; the statement that gives your realization. That statement will bear fruit."

The other day I went into a shop where I know the employer quite well. I had given one of his employees an affirmation card. I said to him, jokingly, "I wouldn't waste an affirmation card on you. You wouldn't use it." He replied, "Oh sure, give me one. I'll use it." The following week I gave him a card. Before I left he rushed up to me excitedly and said, "I made the statement and two new customers walked in." It was: "Now is the appointed time; today is the day of my amazing good fortune." It had clicked.

So many people use their words in exaggerated and reckless statements. I find a great deal of material for my talks in the beauty parlor. A young girl wanted a magazine to read. She called to the operator, "Give me something terribly new and frightfully exciting." All she wanted was the latest moving picture magazine. You hear people say, "I wish something terribly exciting would happen." They are inviting some unhappy, but exciting, experience into their lives. Then they wonder why it happened to them.

There should be a chair of metaphysics in all colleges. Metaphysics is the wisdom of the ages. It is the ancient wisdom taught all through the centuries in India and Egypt and Greece. Hermes Trismegistus was a great teacher of Egypt. His teachings were closely guarded and have come down to us over ten centuries. He lived in Egypt in the days when the present race of men was in its infancy. But if you read the "Kybalion" carefully, you find that he taught just what we are teaching today. He said that all mental states were accompanied by vibrations. You combine with what you vibrate to, so let us all now vibrate to success, happiness and abundance.

Now is the appointed time. Today is the day of my amazing good fortune.

Chapter 6 - The Fork in the Road

"Choose you this day whom ye will serve." --Josh. 24:15

Every day there is a necessity of choice (a fork in the road). "Shall I do this, or shall I do that? Shall I go, or shall I stay?" Many people do not know what to do. They rush about letting other people make decisions for them, then regret having taken their advice.

There are others who carefully reason things out. They weigh and measure the situation like dealing in groceries, and are surprised when they fail to obtain their goal. There are still other people who follow the magic path of intuition and find themselves in their Promised Land in the twinkling of an eye.

Intuition is a spiritual faculty high above the reasoning mind, but on the path is all that you desire or require.

In my book "The Game of Life and How to Play It," I give many examples of success attained through using this marvelous faculty. I say also that prayer is telephoning to God and intuition is God telephoning to you. (Correspondence Course.)

So choose ye this day to follow the magic path of intuition.

In my question and answer classes I tell you how to cultivate intuition. In most people it is a faculty which has remained dormant. So we say, "Awake though that sleepeth. Wake up to your leads and hunches. Wake up to the divinity within!" Claude Bragdon said, "To live intuitively is to live fourth dimensionally."

Now it is necessary for your to make a decision, you face a fork in the road. Ask for a definite unmistakable lead, and you will receive it.

We find many events to interpret metaphysically in the Book of Joshua. "After the death of Moses, the divine command came to Joshua, 'Now therefore, arise, go over the Jordan, thou and all thy people, unto the land which I do give to them. Every place the sole of your feet shall tread upon; to you have I given it'.

The feet are the symbol of understanding, so it means metaphysically all that we understand stands under us in consciousness, and what is rooted there can never be taken from us.

For the Bible goes on to say: "There shall not any man be able to stand before thee all the days of thy life...I will not fail thee, nor forsake thee. Only be thou strong and very courageous, that thou mayest observe to do according to all the law, which Moses my servant commanded thee: "Turn not from it to the right hand or to the left, that thou mayest prosper whithersoever thou goest."

So we find we have success through being strong and very courageous in following spiritual law. We are back again to the "fork in the road" - the necessity of choice.

"Choose you this day whom ye shall serve," the intellect or divine guidance.

A well-known man, who has become a great power in the financial world, said to a friend, "I always follow intuition and I am luck incarnate."

Inspiration (which is divine guidance) is the most important thing in life. People come to Truth meetings for inspiration. I find the right word will start divine activity operating in their affairs.

A woman came to me with a complication of affairs. I said to her, "Let God juggle the situation." It clicked. She took the affirmation, "I now let God juggle this situation." Almost immediately she rented a house, which had been vacant for a long time. Let God juggle every situation, for when you try to juggle the situation, you drop all the balls.

In my question and answer classes, I would be asked, "How do you let God juggle a situation, and what do you mean when you say I should not juggle it?" You juggle with the intellect. The intellect would say, "Times are hard, no activity in real estate. Don't expect anything until the Fall of 1958." With spiritual law there is only the now. Before you call you are answered, for "time and space are but a dream," and your blessing is there waiting for you to release it by faith and the word.

"Choose you this day whom ye will serve," fear or faith.

In every act prompted by fear lies the germ of its own defeat. It takes much strength and courage to trust God. We often trust him in little things, but when it comes to a big situation we feel we had better attend to it ourselves; then comes defeat and failure.

The following extract from a letter which I received from a woman in the West shows how conditions can change in the twinkling of an eye.

"I've had the pleasure of reading your wonderful book, 'The Game of Life and How to Play It.' I have four boys, ten, thirteen, fifteen and seventeen, and thought how wonderful for them to grasp it, in their early life, and be able to get things which are theirs by Divine Right.

"The lady who let me read her copy gave me other things to read, but it seemed when I picked this book up it was magnetic and I could not let go of it. After reading it I realized, I was trying to live Divinely but did not understand the law, or I would have been much further advanced.

"At first I thought it quite hard to find a place in the business world, after so many years of being a mother. But I got this statement, 'God makes a way where there is no way.' And He did that very thing for me.

"I am grateful for my position, and smile when people say, 'How do you do it, manage four growing boys, a home, after all the times you have been hospitalized with such major operations and none of your relatives near you?'"

I have that statement in my book, "God makes a way where there is no way." God made a way for her in business when all her friends said it couldn't be done. The average person will tell you almost anything can't be done.

I had an example of this the other day. In a shop I found a delightful little silver dripolator which would make just one cup of anything. I showed it to some of friends with enthusiasm, thinking it so very cute, and one said, "It will never work." The other said, "If it belonged to me, I'd throw it away." I stood up for the little dripolator and said I knew it would work, which it did.

My friends were simply typical of the average person who says, "It can't be done."

122

All big ideas meet with opposition. Do not let other people rock your boat. Follow the path of wisdom and understanding, "and turn not from it to the right hand or to the left, that thou mayest prosper withersoever thou goest."

In the thirteenth verse of the twenty-fourth Chapter of Joshua, we read a remarkable statement: "And I have given you a land for which ye did not labour, and cities which ye built not, and ye dwell in them; of the vineyards and oliveyards which ye planted not, do ye eat."

This shows that man cannot earn anything, his blessings come as gifts. (Gifts lest any man shall boast.)

With the realization of wealth, we receive the gift of wealth. With the realization of success, we receive the gift of success, for success and abundance are states of mind.

"For it is the Lord our God, he it is, that brought us up, and our fathers out of the land of Egypt, out of the house of bondage." The land of Egypt stands for darkness - the house of bondage, where man is a slave to his doubts and fears, and beliefs in lack and limitation, the result of having followed the wrong fork in the road.

Misfortune is due to failure to stick to the things which spirit has revealed through intuition. All big things have been accomplished by men who stuck to their big ideas. Henry Ford was past middle age when the idea of the Ford car came to him. He had great difficulty in raising the money. His friends thought it was a crazy idea. His father said to him, tearfully, "Henry, why do you give up a good twenty-five dollar a week job in order to chase a crazy idea?" But no one could rock Henry Ford's boat.

So in order to come out of the land of Egypt, out of the land of bondage, we must make the right decisions. Follow the right fork in the road. "Only be thou strong and very courageous, that thou mayest observe to do according to the law, which Moses my servant commanded thee: turn not from it to the right hand nor to the left, that thou mayest prosper whithersoever thou goest."

So, as we reach the fork in the road today, let us fearlessly follow the voice of intuition. The Bible calls it "the still small voice." On this path is the good, already prepared for you. You will find the "land for which ye did not labour, and cities which ye built not, and ye dwell in them; of the vineyards and oliveyards which ye planted not, do ye eat."

I am divinely led, I follow the right fork in the road. God makes a way where there is no way.

Chapter 7 - Crossing Your Red Sea

"Speak unto the children of Israel that they go forward." --Ex. 14:15

One of the most dramatic stories in the Bible is the episode of the children of Israel crossing the Red Sea. Moses was leading them out of the land of Egypt where they were kept in bondage and slavery. They were being pursued by the Egyptians.

The children of Israel, like most people, did not enjoy trusting God; they did a lot of murmuring. They said to Moses: "Is not this the word that we did tell thee in Egypt, saying, Let us alone, that we may serve the Egyptians? For it had been better for us to serve the Egyptians, than that we should die in the wilderness."

"And Moses said unto the people, Fear ye not, stand still, and see the salvation of the lord, which he will show to you today, for the Egyptians whom ye have seen today, ye shall see them again no more forever."

"The Lord shall fight for you, and ye shall hold your peace."

We might say that Moses pounded faith into the children of Israel. They preferred being slaves to their old doubts and fears (for Egypt stands for darkness) than to take the giant swing into faith, and pass through the wilderness to their Promised Land. There is, indeed, a wilderness to pass through before your Promised Land is reached. The old doubts and fears encamp round about you, but there is always someone to tell you to go forward!

There is always a Moses on your pathway. Sometimes it is a friend, sometimes intuition! "And the Lord said to Moses, Wherefore cryest though unto me? Speak unto the children of Israel, that they go forward!" "But lift thou up thy rod, and stretch out thine hand over the sea, and divide it; and the children of Israel shall go on dry ground through the midst of the sea."

"And Moses stretched out his hand over the sea; and the Lord caused the sea to go back by a strong east wind all that night, and made the sea dry land, and the waters were divided." "And the children of Israel went into the midst of the sea upon the dry ground, and the waters were a wall unto them on their right hand, and on their left." "And the Egyptians pursued, and went in after them to the midst of the sea, even all Pharaoh's horses, his chariots, and his horsemen." "And the Lord said unto Moses, Stretch out thine hand over the sea, that the waters may come again upon the Egyptians, upon their chariots, and upon their horsemen." "And Moses stretched forth his hand over the sea, and the sea returned; and the Egyptians fled against it, and the Lord overthrew the Egyptians in the midst of the sea." "And the waters returned, and covered the chariots, and the horsemen, and all the hosts of Pharaoh that came into the sea after them; there remained not so much as one of them."

Now remember, the Bible is talking about the individual. It is talking about your wilderness, your Red Sea, and your Promised Land.

Each one of you has a Promised Land, a heart's desire, but you have been so enslaved by the Egyptians (your negative thoughts), it seems very far away, and too good to be true. You consider trusting God a very risky proposition. The wilderness might prove worse than the Egyptians.

And how do you know your Promised Land really exists? The reasoning mind will always back up the Egyptians. But sooner or later, something says, "Go forward!" It is usually circumstances - you are driven to it.

I give the example of a student. She is a very marvelous pianist and had great success abroad. She came back with a book full of press clippings, and a happy heart. A relative took an interest in her and said she would back her financially for a concert tour. They chose a manager who took charge of the expenses and attended to her bookings. After a concert or two, there were no more funds. The manager had taken them. My friend was left stranded, desolate and disappointed. This was about the time that she came to me. She hated the man, and it was making her ill. She had very little money and could afford only a cheerless room where her hands were often too cold to practice.

She was indeed in bondage to the Egyptians - hate, resentment, lack and limitation. Someone brought her to one of my meetings, and she spoke to me and told her story. I said, "In the first place you must stop hating that man. When you are able to forgive him, your success will come back to you. You are taking your initiation in forgiveness." It seemed a pretty big order, but she tried and came regularly to all my meetings.

In the meantime, the relative had started a suit to recover the money. Time went on and it never came to court. My friend had a call to go to California. She was no longer disturbed by the situation, and had forgiven the man. Suddenly, after about four years, she was notified that the case had come to court. She called me upon her arrival in New York, and asked me to speak the word for rightness and justice. They went at the time appointed, and it was all settled out of court, the man restoring the money by monthly payments.

She came to me overflowing with joy, for she said, "I hadn't the least resentment toward the man. He was amazed when I greeted him cordially." Her relative said that all the money was to go to her, so she found herself with a big bank account.

Now she will soon reach her Promised Land. She came out of the house of bondage (of hate and resentment) and crossed her Red Sea. Her goodwill toward the man caused the waters to part, and she crossed over on dry land.

Dry land symbolizes something substantial under your feet, the feet symbolizing understanding.

Moses stands out as one of the greatest figures in biblical history. It came to Moses to move from Egypt with his nation. The task before him was not only the unwillingness of Pharaoh to let go of those whom he had made into profitable slaves, but also to stimulate to open rebellion this nation which had lost its initiative under the hardships of its taskmasters.

It required extraordinary genius to meet this condition, which Moses possessed with self-abnegation and the courage of his own convictions. Self-abnegation! He was called the meekest of men. We have often heard the expression, "As meek as Moses". He was so meek towards the commands of the Lord that he became one of the strongest of men.

"The Lord said to Moses, 'Lift thou up thy rod, and stretch out thine hand over the sea, and divide it, and the children of Israel shall go on dry ground through the midst of the sea.'" So, never doubting, he said to the children of Israel, "Go forward." This was a daring thing to do, to lead a multiple of people into the sea, having perfect faith they would not drown.

Behold the miracle! "... the Lord caused the sea to go back by a strong east wind all that night, and made the sea dry land, and the waters were divided."

Now remember, this could happen for you this very day. Think of your problem. Maybe you have lost your initiative from living so long a slave to Pharaoh (your doubts, fears and discouragements). Say to yourself, "Go forward."

" ... the Lord caused the sea to go back by a strong east wind." We will think of this strong east wind as a strong affirmation.

Take a vital statement of Truth. For example if your problem is a financial one, say "My supply comes from God, and big happy financial surprises come to me under grace, in perfect ways." The statement is a good one, for it contains the element of mystery.

We are told that God works in mysterious ways His wonders to perform. We might say in surprising ways. Now that you have made your statement for supply, you have caused the east wind to blow.

So walk up to your Red Sea of lack or limitation. The way to walk up to your Red Sea is to do something to show your fearlessness.

I will tell the story of a student who had an invitation to visit friends at a very fashionable summer resort. She had been living in the country for a long time, grown heavier, and nothing fitted her but her girl scout suit. Suddenly, she received the invitation. It meant evening clothes, slippers and accessories, none of which she had, and no money to buy them. She came to me. I said, "What is your hunch?"

She replied, "I feel very fearless. I have the hunch to go anyway." So she squeezed herself into something to travel in and went.

When she arrived at her friend's house she was greeted warmly, but her hostess said, with some embarrassment, "Maybe what I've done will hurt you, but there are some evening clothes and slippers I never wear which I have put in your room. Won't you make use of them?" My friend assured her she would be delighted - and everything fit perfectly. She had, indeed, walked up to her Red Sea and passed over on dry land.

The waters of my Red Sea part, and I pass over on dry land; I now go forward into my Promised Land.

Chapter 8 - The Watchman at the Gate

"Also I set watchmen over you, saying, Hearken to the sound of the trumpet." --Jeremiah 6:17

We must all have a watchman at the gate of our thoughts. The Watchman at the Gate is the superconscious mind. We have the power to choose our thoughts.

Since we have lived in the race thought for thousands of years, it seems almost impossible to control them. They rush through our minds like stampeding cattle or sheep. But a single sheepdog can control the frightened sheep and guide them into the sheep pen.

I saw a picture in the newsreels of a shepherd dog controlling the sheep. He had rounded up all but three. These three resisted and resented. They baahed and lifted their front feet in protest, but the dog simply sat down in front and never took his eyes off them. He did not bark or threaten. He just sat and looked his determination. In a little while the sheep tossed their heads and went in the pen.

We can learn to control our thoughts in the same way, by gentle determination, not force.

We take an affirmation and repeat it continually, while our thoughts are on the rampage. We cannot always control our thoughts, but we can control our words, and repetition impresses the subconscious, and we are then master of the situation.

In the sixth Chapter of Jeremiah we read: "I set a watchman over you, saying, Hearken to the sound of the trumpet."

Your success and happiness in life depend upon the watchman at the gate of your thoughts, sooner or later, crystallize on the external.

People think by running away from a negative situation, they will be rid of it, but the same situation confronts them wherever they go. They will meet the same experiences until they have learned their lessons. This idea is brought out in the moving picture, "The Wizard of Oz."

The little girl, Dorothy, is very unhappy because the mean woman in the village wants to take away her dog, Toto. She goes, in despair, to confide in her Aunt Em and Uncle Henry, but they are too busy to listen, and tell her to "run along."

She says to Toto, "There is somewhere, a wonderful place high above the skies where everybody is happy and no one is mean." How she would love to be there! A Kansas cyclone suddenly comes along, and she and Toto are lifted up, high in the sky, and land in the country of Oz.

Everything seems very delightful at first, but soon she has the same old experiences. The mean old woman of the village has turned into a terrible witch, and is still trying to get Toto from her. How she wishes she could be back in Kansas. She is told to find the Wizard of Oz. He is all powerful and will grant her request.

She starts off to find his palace in the Emerald City. On the way she meets a scarecrow. He is so unhappy because he hasn't a brain. She meets a man made of tin, who is so unhappy because he hasn't a heart. Then she meets a lion who is so unhappy because he has no courage. She cheers them up by saying, "We'll all go to the Wizard of Oz and he'll give what we want" - the scarecrow a brain, the tin man a heart, and the lion courage.

They encounter terrible experiences, for the bad witch is determined to capture Dorothy and take away Toto and the ruby slippers which protect her. At last they reach the Emerald Palace of the Wizard of Oz.

They ask for an audience, but are told no one has ever seen the Wizard of Oz, who lives mysteriously in the palace. But through the influence of the good witch of the North, they enter the palace. There they discover the Wizard is just a fake magician from Dorothy's home town in Kansas. They are all in despair because their wishes cannot be granted!

But then the good witch shows them that their wishes are already granted. The scarecrow has developed a brain by having to decide what to do in the experiences he has encountered, the tin man finds he has a heart because he loves Dorothy, and the lion has become courageous because he had to show courage in his many adventures. The good witch from the North says to Dorothy, "What have you learned from your experiences?" and Dorothy replies, "I have learned that my heart's desire is in my own home and in my own front yard." So the good witch waves her wand, and Dorothy is at home again.

She wakes up and finds that the scarecrow, the tin man, and the lion are the men who work on her uncle's farm. They are so glad to have her back. This story teaches that if you run away your problems will run after you.

Be undisturbed by a situation, and it will fall away of its own weight.

There is an occult law of indifference. "None of these things move me." "None of these things disturb me" we might say in modern language.

When you can no longer be disturbed, all disturbance will disappear from the external.

"I set watchmen over you, saying, Hearken to the sound of the trumpet." A trumpet is a musical instrument, used in olden times to draw people's attention to something - to victory, to order.

You will form the habit of giving attention to every thought and word when you realize their importance.

The imagination, the scissors of the mind, is constantly cutting out the events to come into your life. Many people are cutting out fear-pictures, seeing things which are not divinely planned. With the "single eye," man sees only the Truth. He sees through evil, knowing that out of it comes good. He transmutes injustice into justice, and disarms his seeming enemy by sending good-will.

We read in mythology of the Cyclops, a race of giants, said to have inhabited Sicily. These giants had only one eye in the middle of the forehead. The seat of the imaging faculty is situated in the forehead (between the eyes), so these fabled giants came from this idea.

You are indeed a giant when you have a single eye. Then every thought will be a constructive thought, and every word a word of Power. Let the third eye be the watchman at the gate.

By seeing clearly the perfect plan, we could redeem the world, with our inner eye seeing a world of peace and plenty and goodwill.

"Judge not by appearances, judge righteous judgment." "Nation shall not lift up sword against nation, neither shall they learn war anymore."

The occult law of indifference means that you are undisturbed by adverse appearances. You hold steadily to the constructive thought, which wins out.

Spiritual law transcends the law of Karma.

This is the attitude of mind which must be held by the healer or practitioner towards his patient. Indifferent to appearances of lack, loss or sickness, he brings about the change in mind, body and affairs.

Let me quote from the thirty-first Chapter Jeremiah. The keynote is one of rejoicing. It gives a picture of the individual freed from negative thinking.

"For there shall be a day that the watchmen upon the mount Ephraim shall cry, Arise ye, and let us go up to Zion unto the Lord our God."

The Watchman at the Gate neither slumbers nor sleeps. It is the "Eye which watches over Israel."

But the individual, living in a world of negative thought, is not conscious of this inner eye. He may occasionally have flashes of intuition or illumination, then falls back into a world of chaos. It takes determination and eternal vigilance to check up on words and thoughts. Thoughts of fear, failure, resentment and ill-will must be dissolved and dissipated.

Take the statement: "Every plant my father in heaven has not planted shall be rooted up." This gives you a vivid picture of rooting up weeds in a garden. They are thrown aside, and dry up because they are without soil to nourish them.

You nourish negative thoughts by giving them your attention. Use the occult law of indifference and refuse to be interested. Soon you will starve out the "army of all aliens." Divine ideas will crowd your consciousness, false ideas fade away, and you will desire only that which God desires through you.

The Chinese have a proverb, "The philosopher leaves the cut of his coat to the tailor." But the individual, living in a world of negative thought, is not conscious of this inner eye. So leave the plan of your life to the Divine Designer, and you will find all conditions permanently perfect.

The ground I am on is holy ground. I now expand rapidly into the divine plan of my life, where all conditions are permanently perfect.

Chapter 9 - The Way of Abundance

"Then shalt thou lay up gold as dust." --Job 22:24

The way of abundance is a one-way street. As the old saying is, "There are no two ways about it." You are either heading for lack, or heading for abundance. The man with a rich consciousness and the man with a poor consciousness are not walking on the same mental street.

There is a lavish supply, divinely planned for each individual. The rich man is tapping it, for rich thoughts produce rich surroundings.

Change your thoughts, and in the twinkling of an eye, all your conditions change. Your world is a world of crystallized ideas, crystallized words. Sooner or later, you reap the fruits of your words and thoughts.

"Words are bodies or forces which move spirally and return in due season to cross the lives of their creators."

People who are always talking lack and limitation, reap lack and limitation. You cannot enter the Kingdom of Abundance bemoaning your lot.

I know a woman who had always been limited in her ideas of prosperity. She was continually making her old clothes "do," instead of buying new clothes. She was very careful of what money she had, and was always advising her husband not to spend so much. She said repeatedly, "I don't want anything I can't afford." She couldn't afford much, so she didn't have much.

Suddenly her whole world cracked up. Her husband left her, weary of her nagging and limited thoughts. She was in despair, when one day she came across a book on metaphysics. It explained the power of thought and words. She realized that she had invited every unhappy experience by wrong thinking. She laughed heartily at her mistakes, and decided to profit by them. She determined to prove the law of abundance.

She used what money she had, fearlessly, to show her faith in her invisible supply. She relied upon God as the source of her prosperity. She no longer voiced lack and limitation. She kept herself feeling and looking prosperious.

Her old friends scarcely recognized her. She had swung into the way of abundance. More money came to her than she had ever had before. Unheard-of doors opened; amazing channels were freed. She became very successful in a work she had had no training for. She found herself on miracle ground. What had happened?

133

She had changed the quality of her words and thoughts. She had taken God into her confidence, and into all her affairs. She had many eleventh hour demonstrations, but her supply always came, for she dug her ditches and gave thanks without wavering.

Someone called me up recently and said, "I am looking desperately for a position."

I replied, "Don't look desperately for it, look for it with praise and thanksgiving, forGod said to pray with praise and thanksgiving."

Praise and thanksgiving open the gates, for expectancy always wins.

Of course, the law is impersonal, and a dishonest person with rich thoughts will attract riches, but "a thing ill-got has ever bad success," as Shakespeare says. It will be of short duration and will not bring happiness.

We have only to read the papers to see that the way of the transgressor is hard.

That is the reason it is so necessary to make your demands aright on the Universal Supply and ask for what is yours by divine right and under grace in a perfect way.

Some people attract prosperity, but cannot hold it. Sometimes their heads are turned, sometimes they lose it through fear and worry.

A friend in one of my question and answer classes told this story. Some people in his hometown, who had always been poor, suddenly struck oil in their back yard. It brought great riches. The father joined the country club and went in for golf. He was no longer young - the exercise was too much for him and he dropped dead on the links.

This filled the whole family with fear. They all decided they might have heart trouble, so they are now in bed with trained nurses watching every heart beat.

In the race-thought people must worry about something. They no longer worried about money, so they shifted their worries to health. The old idea was, "that you can't have everything." If you got one thing, you'd lose another. People were always saying, "Your luck won't last," "It's too good to be true."

In the superconscious, there is a lavish supply for every demand, and your good is perfect and permanent.

What a picture of opulence! With the average person (who has thought in terms of lack for a long time) it is very difficult to build up a rich consciousness.

I have a student who has attracted great success by making the statement: "I am the daughter of the King! My rich Father now pours out his abundance upon me. I am the daughter of the King! Everything makes way for me."

Many people put up with limited conditions because they are too lazy (mentally), to think themselves out of them. You must have a great desire for financial freedom, you must feel yourself rich, you must see yourself rich, you must continually prepare for riches. Become as a little child and make believe you are rich. You are then impressing the subconscious with expectancy.

The imagination is man's workshop, the scissors of the mind, where he is constantly cutting out the events of his life!

The superconscious is the realm of inspiration, revelation, illumination and intuition. Intuition is usually known as a hunch. I do not apologize for the word "hunch" anymore. It is now in Webster's latest dictionary. I had a hunch to look up "hunch," and there it was.

The superconscious is the realm of perfect ideas. The great genius captures his thoughts from the superconscious.

"Without the vision (imagination) my people perish." When people have lost the power to image their good, they "perish" (or go under).

It is interesting to compare the translation of the French and English Bibles. In the 21st verse of the 22nd Chapter of Job we read: "Acquaint now thyself with him, and be at peace, thereby good shall come unto thee."

In the French Bible we read: "Attach thyself to God and you will have peace. Thou shalt thus enjoy happiness." The 23rd verse: "If thou return to the Almighty, thou shalt be build up, thou shalt put away iniquity far from thy tabernacles." In the French translation we read: "Thou shalt be re-established if thou returnest to the Almighty, putting iniquity far off from your dwellings."

In the 24th verse we read a new and amazing translation. The English Bible reads, "Then shalt thou lay up gold as dust, and the gold of Ophir as the stones of the brooks." The French Bible says: "Throw gold into the dust, the gold of Ophir amongst the pebbles of the torrents, and the Almighty shall be thy gold, thy silver, thy riches."

This means if people are depending entirely on their visible supply, it is even better to throw it away and trust absolutely to the Almighty for gold, silver and riches.

I give an example in the story told me by a friend. A priest went to visit a nunnery in France, where they fed many children. One of the nuns, in despair, told the priest they had no food, the children must go hungry. She said that they had but one piece of silver (about the value of a quarter of a dollar). They needed food and clothing.

The priest said, "Give me the coin." She handed it to him and he threw

it out the window.

"Now," he said, "rely entirely upon God." Within a short time friends arrived with plenty of food and gifts of money.

This doesn't mean to throw away what money you have, but don't depend upon it. Depend upon your invisible supply, the Bank of the Imagination.

Let us now attach ourselves to God and have peace. For He shall be our gold, our silver and our riches.

The inspiration of the Almighty shall be my defense and I shall have plenty of silver.

Chapter 10 - I Shall Never Want

"The Lord is my Shepherd; I shall not want." --Psalms 23:1

The 23rd Psalm is the best known of all the Psalms - we might say that it is the keynote to the message of the Bible. It tells man he shall never want, when he has the realization (or conviction) that the Lord is his Shepherd; the realization that Infinite Intelligence supplies every need.

If you get this conviction today, every need will be met now and forevermore. You will draw, instantly, from the abundance of the spheres, whatever you desire or require; for what you need is already on your pathway.

A woman suddenly had the realization: "The Lord is my Shepherd, I shall never want." She seemed to be touching her invisible supply, she felt outside of Time and Space, she no longer relied on the external. Her first demonstration was a small, but necessary one. She needed at once some large paperclips, but had no time to go to the stationers to buy them. In looking for something else, she opened a little-used chest, and in it she found about a dozen large paperclips. She felt that the law was working, and gave thanks; then some needed money appeared. Things large and small came her way.

Since then she has relied upon the statement: "The Lord is my Shepherd, I shall never want."

We used to hear people say, "I do not think it is right to ask God for money or things." They did not realize that this Creative Principle is within each man. True Spirituality is proving God as your supply daily, not just once in awhile.

With this realization, all hoarding and saving would disappear. This does not mean that you should not have a bank account and investments, but it does mean that you should not depend upon them, for if you had a loss in one direction, you would have a gain in another. Always "your barns would be full and your cup flow over."

Now, how does one make this contact with his invisible supply? By taking a statement of Truth which clicks and gives him realization. This is not open to a chosen few, "Whosoever calleth on the name of the Lord shall be delivered." The Lord is your shepherd and my shepherd and everybody's shepherd.

God is the Supreme Intelligence devoted to supplying man's need; the explanation is, that man is God in action. We might say, "I and the great Creative Principle of the Universe are one and the same."

Man only lacks when he loses his contact with this Creative Principle, which must be fully trusted, for it is Pure Intelligence and knows the way of Fulfillment.

The reasoning mind will cause a short circuit. "Trust in me and I will bring it to pass."

Most people are filled with apprehension and dread when there is nothing to cling to on the external.

A woman came to a practitioner and said, "I'm only a poor little woman with no one but God back of me." The practitioner said, "You need not worry if you have God back of you," for "all that the Kingdom affords is yours."

A woman called me on the phone and said, almost in tears, "I'm so worried about the business situation." I replied, "The situation with God remains the same: The Lord is your Shepherd, you shall not want." "If one door shuts, another door opens."

A very successful businessman who conducts all affairs on Truth methods said, "The trouble with most people is that they get to relying on certain conditions. They haven't enough imagination to go forward - to open new channels."

Nearly every big success is built upon a failure.

I was told that Edgar Bergen lost his part in a Broadway production because they did not want any more dummies. Noel Coward got him on the Rudy Vallee radio hour, and he and Charlie McCarthy became famous overnight.

I told the story at one of my meetings of a man who was so poor and discouraged that he ended it all. A few days later came a letter notifying him that he had inherited a large fortune.

A man in the meeting said, "That means, when you want to be dead, your demonstration is three days off." Yes, do not be fooled by the darkness before the dawn.

It is a good thing to see the dawn once in a while, to convince you how unfailing it is. It reminds me of an experience of several years ago. I had a friend who lived in Brooklyn near Prospect Park. She liked to do unusual things and said to me, "Come to visit me and we'll get up early and see the sunrise in Prospect Park."

At first I refused, and then came the hunch that it would be an interesting experience. It was in the summer. We got up about four o'clock, my friend, her little daughter and myself. It was pitch dark, but we sallied forth down the street, to the entrance of the Park. Some policemen eyed us curiously, but my friend said to them with dignity, "We are going to see the sunrise" and it seemed to satisfy them. We walked through the park to the beautiful rose garden.

A faint pink streak apppeared in the East, then suddenly we heard a most tremendous uproar. We were near the Zoo and all the animals were greeting the dawn. The lions and tigers roared, the hyenas laughed, there were shrieks and howls, every animal had something to say for a new day was at hand.

It was indeed most inspiring. The light slanted through the trees; everything had an unearthly aspect. Then, as it grew lighter, our shadows were in front instead of behind us: The dawn of a new day!

This is the wonderful dawn which comes to each one of us after some darkness. Your dawn of Success, Happiness and Abundance is sure to come.

Every day is important, for we read in the wonderful Sanskrit poem, "Look well, therefore, to this day, such is the salutation of the dawn." This day the Lord is your Shepherd! This day, you shall not want, as you and this great Creative Principle are one and the same.

The 34th Psalm is also a Psalm of security. It starts with a blessing for the Lord, "I will bless the Lord at all times, His praise shall continually be in my mouth."

They that seek the Lord shall not want any good thing." Seeking the Lord means that man must make the first move. "Draw near to me and I will draw near to thee, saith the Lord." You seek the Lord by making your affirmations, expecting and preparing for your good. If you ask for success and prepare for failure, you will receive the thing you have prepared for.

I tell in my book, "The Game of Life and How to Play It," of a man who asked me to speak the word that all his debts be wiped out. After the treatment, he said, "Now I'm thinking what I'll say to the people when I haven't the money to pay them." A treatment won't help you if you haven't faith in it, for faith and expectancy impresses the subconscious mind with the picture of fulfillment.

In the 23rd Psalm we read, "He restoreth my soul." Your soul is your subconscious mind and must be restored with the right ideas.

Whatever you feel deeply is impressed upon the subconscious and manifests in your affairs. If you are convinced that you are a failure, you will be a failure, until you impress the subconscious with the conviction you are a success. This is done by making an affirmation which "clicks."

A friend in a meeting said that I had given her the statement as she was leaving the room, "The ground you are on is harvest ground." Things with her had been very dull, but this statement clicked.

"Harvest Ground, Harvest Ground", rang in her ears. Good things immediately commenced to come to her, and happy surprises.

The reason it is necessary to make an affirmation is because repetition impresses the subconscious. You cannot control your thoughts at first, but you can control your words. Every day choose the right words, the right thoughts!

The Imaging faculty is the creative faculty, "Out of the imaginations of the heart come the issues of life."

We have all a bank we can draw upon, the Bank of the Imagination. Let us imagine ourselves rich, well and happy. Imagine all our affairs are in divine order, but leave the way of fulfillment to Infinite Intelligence. "He has weapons ye know not of." He has channels which will surprise you.

One of the most important passages in the 23rd Psalm is, "Thou preparest a table before me in the presence of mine enemies." This means that even in the presence of the enemy situation, brought on by your doubts, fears or resentments, a way out is prepared for you.

The Lord is my Shepherd, I shall never want.

Chapter 11 - Look With Wonder

"I will remember the works of the Lord; surely I will remember thy wonders of old." --Psalms 77:11

The words 'wonder' and 'wonderful' are used many times in the Bible. In the dictionary the word 'wonder' is defined as, "a cause for surprise, astonishment, a miracle, a marvel."

Ouspensky, in his book, "Tertium Organum," calls the 4th dimensional world, the "World of the Wondrous." He has figured out mathematically that there is a realm where all conditions are perfect.

We might say, "Seek ye first the world of the wondrous, and all things shall be added unto you." It can only be reached through a state of consciousness.

The future holds promises of mysterious good. Anything can happen overnight. Robert Louis Stevenson, in "A Child's Garden of Verses" says: "The world is so full of a number of things. I'm sure we should all be as happy as kings." So let us look with wonder at that which is before us.

That statement was given me a number of years ago, and I mention it in my book, "The Game of Life and How To Play It." I had missed an opportunity and felt that I should have been more awake to my good. The next day, I took the statement early in the morning, "I look with wonder at that which is before me."

At noon the phone rang, and the proposition was put to me again. This time I grasped it. I did indeed look with wonder for I never expected the opportunity to come to me again.

A friend in one of my meetings said the other day, that this statement had brought her wonderful results. It fills the consciousness with happy expectancy.

Children are filled with happy expectancy until grownup people and unhappy experiences bring them out of the world of the wondrous! Let us look back and remember some of the gloomy ideas which were given us: "Eat the speckled apples first." "Don't expect too much, then you won't be disappointed." "You can't have everything in this life." "Childhood is your happiest time." "No one knows what the future will bring." What a start in life!

These are some of the impressions I picked up in early childhood. At the age of six I had a great sense of responsibility. Instead of looking with wonder at that which was before me, I looked with fear and suspicion. I feel much younger now than I did when I was six. I have an early photograph taken about that time, grasping a flower, but with a care-worn and hopeless expression. I had left the world of the wondrous behind me! I was now living in the world of realities, as my elders told me and it was far from wondrous.

It is a great privilege for children to live in this age, when they are taught Truth from their birth. Even if they are not taught actual metaphysics, the ethers are filled with joyous expectancy. You may become a Shirley Temple or a Freddy Bartholomew or a great pianist at the age of six and go on a concert tour.

We are all now back in the world of the wondrous, where anything can happen overnight, for when miracles do come, they come quickly!

So let us become Miracle Conscious and prepare for miracles, expect miracles, and we are then inviting them into our lives.

Maybe you need a financial miracle! There is a supply for every demand. Through active faith, the word and intuition, we release this invisible supply.

I will give an example: One of my students found herself almost without funds; she needed one thousand dollars, and she had had plenty of money at one time and beautiful possessions, but had nothing left but an ermine wrap. No fur dealer would give her much for it.

I spoke the word that it would be sold to the right person for the right price, or that the supply would come in some other way. It was necessary that the money manifest at once; it was no time to worry or reason.

She was on the street making her affirmations. It was a stormy day. She said to herself, "I'm going to show active faith in my invisible supply by taking a taxi cab." It was a very strong hunch. As she got out of the taxi, at her destination, a woman stood waiting to get in. It was an old friend, a very, very kind friend. It was the first time in her life she had ever taken a taxi, but her Rolls Royce was out of commission that afternoon.

They talked and my friend told her about the ermine wrap. "Why," her friend said, "I will give you a thousand dollars for it." And that afternoon she had the cheque.

God's ways are ingenious, His methods are sure.

A student wrote me the other day that she was using that statement -"God's ways are ingenious, His methods are sure." A series of unexpected contacts brought about a situation she had been desiring. She looked with wonder at the working of the law.

Our demonstrations usually come within a "split second." All is timed with amazing accuracy in Divine Mind. My student left the taxi, just as her friend stopped to enter; a second later, she would have hailed another taxi.

Man's part is to be wide awake to his leads and hunches; for on the magic path of Intuition is all that he desires or requires.

In Moulton's Modern Reader's Bible, the book of Psalms is recognized as the perfection of lyric poetry.

"The musical meditation which is the essence of lyrics can find no higher field than the devout spirit which at once raises itself to the service of God, and overflows on the various sides of active and contemplative life." The Psalms are also human documents, and I have selected the 77th Psalm because it gives the picture of a man in despair, but as he contemplates the wonders of God, faith and assurance are restored to him.

"I cried unto God with my voice, even unto God with my voice; and He gave ear unto me.

In the day of my trouble I sought the Lord, my soul refused to be comforted.
Will the Lord cast off forever? And will he be favourable no more? Hath God forgotten to be gracious? Hath he in anger shut up his tender mercies?
And I said, This is my infirmity, but I will remember the years of the right hand of the Most High.

I will meditate also of all thy work, and talk of thy doings.

Thy way, O God, is in the sanctuary, who is so great a God as our God! Thou art the God that doest wonders.

Thou hast with thine arm redeemed thy people."

This is a picture of what the average Truth student goes through when confronted with a problem. He is assailed by thoughts of doubt, fear and despair. Then some statement of Truth will flash into his consciousness - "God's ways are ingenious, His methods are sure!" He remembers other difficulties which have been overcome, his confidence in God returns. He thinks, "What God has done before, He will do for me and more!"

I was talking to a friend not long ago who said, "I would be pretty dumb if I didn't believe God could solve my problem. So many times before, wonderful things have come to me, I know they will come again!"

So the summing up of the 77th Psalm is, "What God has done before, he now does for me and more!"

It is a good thing to say when you think of your past success, happiness or wealth. All loss comes from your own vain imaginings, fear of loss crept into your conscousness, you carried burdens and fought battles, you reasoned instead of sticking to the magic path of intuition. But in the twinkling of an eye, all will be restored to you.

Now to go back to the child's state of consciousness. You should be filled with wonder, but be careful not to live in your past childhood. I know people who can only think about their happy childhood days. They remember what they wore! No skies have since been so blue, or grass so green. They therefore miss the opportunities of the wonderful now.

I will tell an amusing story of a friend who lived in a town when she was very young, then moved away to another city. She always looked back to the house they first lived in; to her it was an enchanged palace, large, spacious and glamorous. Many years after, when she had grown up, she had an opportunity of visiting this house. She was disillusioned - she found it small, stuffy and ugly. Her idea of beauty had entirely changed, for in the front yard was an iron dog. If you went back to your past, it would not be the same. So in this friend's family they called living in the past, "iron dogging."

Her sister told me a story of some "iron dogging" she had done. When she was about sixteen, she met abroad a very dashing and romantic young man, an artist. This romance didn't last long, but she talked about it a lot to the man she afterwards married.

Years rolled by, the dashing and romantic young man had become a well-known artist and came to this country to have an exhibition of his pictures. My friend was filled with excitement, and hunted him up to renew their friendship. She went to his exhibition, and in walked a portly businessman. No trace was left of the dashing romantic youth! When she told her husband, all he said was, "iron dogging."

Remember, now is the appointed time! Today is the day! And your good can happen overnight.

Look with wonder at that which is before you!

Now let each one think of the good which seems so difficult to attain. It may be health, wealth, happiness or perfect self-expression. Do not think how your good can be accomplished, just give thanks that you have already received on the invisible plane, "therefore the steps leading up to it are secured also."

Be wide awake to your intuitive leads, and suddenly, you find yourself in your Promised Land.

"I look with wonder at that which is before me."

Chapter 12 - Catch Up With Your Good

"And it shall come to pass, that before they call, I will answer; and while they are yet speaking, I will hear." --Isaiah 65:24

Catch up with your good! This is a new way of saying, "Before they call, I will answer."

Your good precedes you; it gets there before you do. But how to catch up with your good? For you must have ears that hear, and eyes that see, or it will escape you.

Some people never catch up with their good in life; they will say, "My life has always been one of hardship, no good luck ever comes to me." They are the people who have been asleep to their opportunities, or through laziness haven't caught up with their good.

A woman told a group of friends that she had not eaten for three days. They dashed about asking people to give her work, but she refused it. She explained that she never got up until twelve o'clock, she liked to lie in bed and read magazines. She just wanted people to support her while she read "Vogue" and "Harper's Bazaar." We must be careful not to slip into lazy states of mind.

Take the affirmation, "I am wide awake to my good, I never miss a trick." Most people are only half awake to their good.

A student said to me, "If I don't follow my hunches, I always get into a jam."

146

I will tell the story of a woman, one of my students, who followed her intuitive leads which brought amazing results. She had been asked to visit friends in a nearby town. She had very little money. When she arrived at her destination, she found the house locked up. They had gone away. She was filled with despair, then commenced to pray. She said, "Infinite Intelligence, give me a definite lead, let me know just what to do!"

The name of a certain hotel flashed into her consciousness. It persisted; the name seemed to stand out in big letters. She had just enough money to get back to New York and the hotel. As she was about to enter, an old friend suddenly appeared who greeted her warmly and whom she hadn't seen in years. She explained that she was living at the hotel but was going away for several months, and added, "Why don't you live in my suite while I am away, it won't cost your a cent." My friend accepted gratefully, and looked with amazement on the working of Spiritual Law. She had caught up with her good by following intuition.

All going forward comes from desire. Science today is going back to Lamarck and his "wishing theory." He claims that birds do not fly because they have wings, but they have wings because they wanted to fly; the result of the "push of the emotional wish."

Think of the irresistible power of thought with clear vision. Many people are in a fog most of the time, making wrong decisions and going the wrong way.

During the Christmas rush, my maid said to a saleswoman at one of the big shops, "I suppose this is your busiest day." She replied, "Oh no! The day after Christmas is our busiest day, when people bring most of the things back." Hundreds of people choosing the wrong gifts because they were not listening to their intuitive leads.

No matter what you are doing, ask for guidance. It saves time and energy and often a lifetime of misery. All suffering comes from the violation of intuition. Unless intuition builds the house, they labor in vain who build it.

Get the habit of hunching, then you will always be on the magic path.

147

"And it shall come to pass, that before they call, I will answer, and while they are yet speaking, I will hear."

Working with spiritual law, we are bringing to pass that which already is. In the Universal Mind it is there as an idea, but is crystallized on the external by a sincere desire.

The idea of a bird was a perfect picture in divine mind. The fish caught the idea, and wished themselves into birds.Are your desires bringing you wings? We should all be bringing some seemingly impossible thing to pass.

One of my affirmations is, "The unexpected happens, my seemingly impossible good now comes to pass."

Do not magnify obstacles, magnify the Lord - that means, magnify God's power. The average person will dwell on all the obstacles and hindrances which are there to prevent his good coming to pass. You "combine with what you notice," so if you give obstacles and hindrances your undivided attention, they grow worse and worse.

Give God your undivided attention. Keep saying silently (in the face of obstacles), "God's ways are ingenious, His methods are sure."

God's power is invicible, (though invisible). "Call unto me and I will answer thee, and show thee great and mighy things which though knowest not."

In demonstrating our good, we must look away from adverse appearances, "Judge not by appearances."

Get some statement which will give you a feeling of assurance, "The long arm of God reaches out over people and conditions, controlling the situation and protecting my interests!"

I was asked to speak the word for a man who was to have a business interview with a seemingly unscrupulous person. I used the statement and rightness and justice came out of the situation at just the exact time I was speaking.

We have all heard the quotation from Proverbs, "Hope deferred maketh the heart grow sick, but when the desire cometh, it is a tree of life."

In desiring sincerely (without anxiety), we are catching up with the thing desired and the desire becomes crystallized on the external. "I will give to you the righteous desire of your heart." Selfish desires - desires which harm others - always return to harm the sender. The righteous desire might be called an echo from the Infinite. It is already a perfect idea in divine mind.

All inventors catch up with the ideas of the articles they invent. I say in my book, "The Game of Life", the telephone was seeking Bell. Often two people discover the same inventions at the same time. They have tuned in with the same idea.

The most important thing in life is to bring the divine plan to pass. Just as the picture of the oak is in the acorn, the divine design of your life is in your superconscious mind, and you must work out the perfect pattern in your affairs. You will then lead a magic life, for in the divine design all conditions are permanently perfect.

People defy the divine design when they are asleep to their good. Perhaps the woman who liked to lie in bed most of the day and read magazines should be writing for magazines, but her habits of laziness dulled all desire to go forward. The fishes who desired wings were alert and alive; they did not spend their days on the bed of the ocean reading "Vogue" and "Harper's Bazaar."

Awake thou that sleepeth and catch up with your good!

"Call on me and I will answer thee, and show thee great and might things, which thou knowest not."

"I now catch up with my good, for before I called I was answered."

Chapter 13 - Rivers in the Desert

"Behold, I will do a new thing: now it shall spring forth; shall ye not know it? I will even make a way in the wilderness, and rivers in the desert." --Isaiah 43:19

In this 43rd Chapter of Isaiah, are many wonderful statements, showing the irresistible power of Supreme Intelligence coming to man's rescue in times of trouble. No matter how impossible the situation seems, Infinite Intelligence knows the way out.

Working with God-Power, man becomes unconditioned and absolute. Let us get a realization of this hidden power that we can call upon at any moment. Make your contact with Infinite Intelligence, (the God within) and all appearance of evil evaporates, for it comes from man's "vain imaginings."

In my question and answer class I would be asked, "How do you make a conscious contact with this Invincible Power?"

In reply, "By your word." "By your word you are justified." As I always say, take a statement which "clicks," that means, gives you a feeling of security.

People are enslaved by ideas of lack; lack of love, lack of money, lack of companionship, lack of health, and so on. They are enslaved by the ideas of interference and incompletion. It is almost impossible to see clearly, your good, for yourself; that is where the healer, practitioner or friend is necessary. Most successful men say they have succeeded because their wives believed in them.

I will quote from a current newspaper, giving Walter P. Chrysler's tribute to his wife. "Nothing," he once said, "has given me more satisfaction in life than the way my wife had faith in me from the very first, through all those years." Chrysler wrote of her, "It seemed to me I could not make anyone understand that I was ambitious except Della. I could tell her and she would nod. It seems to me I even dared to tell her that I intended, some day, to be a master mechanic." She always backed his ambitions.

Talk about your affairs as little as possible, and then only to the ones who will give you encouragement and inspiration. The world is full of "wet blankets," people who will tell you "it can't be done, that you are aiming too high."

As people sit in Truth meetings and services, often a word or an idea will open a way in the wilderness.

Of course the Bible is speaking of states of consciousness. You are in a wilderness or desert when you are out of harmony - when you are angry, resentful, fearful or undecided. Indecision is the cause of much ill health, being unable to make up your mind.

One day when I was in a bus, a woman stopped it and asked the conductor its destination. He told her, but she was undecided. She got half way on, and then got off, then on again. The conductor turned to her and said, "Lady, make up your mind!"

So it is with so many people: "Ladies, make up your minds!"

The intuitive person is never undecided; he is given his leads and hunches, and goes boldly ahead, knowing he is on the magic path. In Truth, we always ask for definite leads just what to do; you will always receive one if you ask for it. Sometimes it comes as intuition, sometimes from the external.

One of my students, named Ada, was walking down the street, undecided whether to go to a certain place or not. She asked for a lead. Two women were walking in front of her. One turned to the other and said, "Why don't you go, Ada?" The woman's name just happened to be Ada. My friend took it as a definite lead and went on to her destination, and the outcome was very successful.

We really lead magic lives, guided and provided for at every step if we have ears to hear and eyes that see. Of course we have left the plane of the intellect and are drawing from the superconscious, the God within, which says, "This is the way, walk ye in it."

Whatever you should know will be revealed to you. Whatever you lack will be provided! "Thus saith the Lord which maketh a way in the sea and a path in the mighty waters."

"Remember ye not the former things, neither consider the things of old."

People who live in the past have severed their contact with the wonderful now. God knows only the now. Now is the appointed time, today is the day.

Many people lead lives of limitation, hoarding and saving, afraid to use what they have, which brings more lack and more limitation.

I give the example of a woman who lived in a small country town. She could scarcely see to get about, and had very little money. A kind friend took her to an oculist and presented her with glasses which enabled her to see perfectly. Sometime later she met her on the street without the glasses. She exclaimed, "Where are your glasses?"

The woman replied, "Well, you don't expect me to hack 'em out by using them every day, do you? I only wear them on Sundays."

You must live in the now and be wide awake to your opportunities.

"Behold, I will do a new thing, now it shall spring forth; shall ye not know it? I will even make a way in the wilderness, and rivers in the desert."

This message is meant for the individual. Think of your problem and know that Infinite Intelligence knows the way of fulfillment. I say 'the way', for before you called you were answered. The supply always precedes the demand.

God is the Giver and the Gift and now creates His own amazing channels.

When you have asked for the Divine Plan of your life to manifest, you are protected from getting the things that are not in the Divine Plan.

You may think that all your happiness depends upon obtaining one particular thing in life; later on, you praise the Lord that you didn't get it.

Sometimes you are tempted to follow the reasoning mind and argue with your intuitive leads. Suddenly the Hand of Destiny pushes you into your right place, and under grace, you find yourself back on the magic path again.

You are now wide awake to your good, you have the ears that hear (your intuitive leads), and the eyes which see the open road of fulfillment.

"The genius withing me is released. I now fulfill my destiny."

Chapter 14 - The Inner Meaning of Snow White and the Seven Dwarfs

I have been asked to give a Metaphysical interpretation of Snow White and the Seven Dwarfs, one of Grimm's Fairy Tales. It is amazing how this picture, a fairy story, swept sophisticated New York and the whole country due to Walt Disney's genius.

This fairytale was supposed to be for children, but men and women have packed the theatre. It is because fairytales come down from old legends of Persia, India and Egypt, which are founded on Truth.

Snow White, the little Princess, has a cruel stepmother, who is jealous of her. This cruel stepmother idea appears also in "Cinderalla." Nearly everyone has a cruel stepmother.

THE CRUEL STEPMOTHER IS A NEGATIVE THOUGHT-FORM YOU HAVE BUILT UP IN THE SUBCONSCIOUS.

Snow White's cruel stepmother is jealous of her and always keeps her in rags and in the background.

ALL CRUEL THOUGHT FORMS DO THIS.

The cruel stepmother consults her magic mirror every day, saying: "Magic mirror on the wall, who is the fairest of them all?" One day the mirror replies: "Thou Queen, mayst fair and beauteous be, but Snow White is lovelier far than thee." This enrages the Queen, so she decides to send Snow White to the forest to be killed by one of her servants. However, the servant's heart melts when Snow White begs for her life, so he leaves her in the woods. The woods are filled with terrifying animals and many pitfalls and dangers. She falls in terror to the ground, and while there, a most unusual spectacle presents itself. Scores of the most delightful little animals and birds creep up and surround her. Rabbits, squirrels, deer, beavers, racoons, etc. She opens her eyes and greets them with pleasure; they are so friendly and attractive. She tells her story and they lead her to a little house which she makes her home.

NOW THESE FRIENDLY BIRDS AND ANIMALS SYMBOLIZE OUR INTUITIVE LEADS OR HUNCHES, WHICH ARE ALWAYS READY TO "GET YOU OUT OF THE WOODS."

The little house proves to be the home of the Seven Dwarfs. Everything is in disorder, so Snow White and her animal friends begin to clean the house. The squirrels dust with their tails, the birds hang things up, using the little deer's horns for a hat-rack. When the seven dwarfs come home from their work of digging gold, they discover the change and at last find Snow White asleep on one of the beds. In the morning she tells her story, remains with them to keep house and cook their meals, and is very happy.

THE SEVEN DWARFS SYMBOLIZE THE PROTECTIVE FORCES ALL ABOUT US.

In the meantime, the cruel stepmother consults her mirror and it says to her: "Over the hills in the green woodshed, where the Seven Dwarfs their dwelling have made, there Snow White is hiding her head, and she is lovelier far, oh, Queen than thee." This infuriates the Queen; so she starts off disguised as an old hag, with a poisoned apple for Snow White.

She finds her in the house of the Seven Dwarfs and tempts her with the big, red luscious apple. The birds and animals endeavor to tell her not to touch it.

THEY TRY TO GIVE HER THE HUNCH NOT TO EAT IT.

They rush around in dismay, but Snow White can't resist the apple, she takes one bite and falls, apparently dead. Now all the little birds and animals rush off to bring the Seven Dwarfs to the rescue; but too late, Snow White lies lifeless. They all bow their little heads in grief. Then suddenly the Prince appears, kisses Snow White, and she comes to life. They are married and live happily ever after. The Queen, the cruel stepmother, is swept away by a terrific storm.

THE OLD THOUGHT-FORM IS DISSOLVED AND DISSIPATED

FOREVER. THE PRINCE SYMBOLIZES THE DIVINE PLAN OF YOUR LIFE. WHEN IT WAKES YOU UP YOU LIVE HAPPILY EVER AFTER.

This is the fairy story which has enthralled New York and the whole country.

Find out what form of tyranny your cruel stepmother is taking in your subconscious. It is some negative conviction which works out in all your affairs.

We hear people saying: "My good always comes to me too late." "I've lost so many opportunities!" We must reverse the thought and say repeatedly: "I am wide awake to my good; I never miss a trick."

WE MUST DROWN OUT THE DREARY SUGGESTIONS OF THE CRUEL STEPMOTHER. ETERNAL VIGILANCE IS THE PRICE OF FREEDOM FROM THESE NEGATIVE THOUGHT-FORMS.

Nothing can hinder, nothing can delay the manifestation of the Divine Plan of my life,

The Light of Lights streams on my pathway, revealing the Open Road of Fulfillment!

The Power of the Spoken Word

FOREWARD

Florence Scovel Shinn taught metaphysics in New York for many years. Her meetings were well attended and in that way she was the means of bringing the message to a considerable number of people.

Her books have had a wide circulation not only in America but abroad. They seem to have a knack of finding their way to remote and unexpected places in Europe and other parts of the world. Now and again we meet someone who came into Truth through finding a Florence Shinn book in the most improbable location.

One secret of her success was that she was always herself: colloquial, informal, friendly, and humorous. She never sought to be literary, conventional, or impressive. For this reason she appealed to thousands who would not have taken the spiritual message through the more conservative and dignified forms, or have been willing to read, at least in the beginning, the standard metaphysical books.

She herself was very spiritual, although this was usually hidden behind a matter of fact and carefree treatment of her subject. The technical or academic approach was not for her. She taught by familiar, practical, and everyday examples.

She had been by profession an artist and book illustrator before becoming a Truth teacher, and belonged to an old Philadelphia family.

She left a collection of notes and memoranda which have been made into the present book. May it have a wide circulation.

Emmet Fox

Chapter 1 - WEAPONS YE KNOW NOT OF

"I have weapons ye know not of! I have ways ye know not of! I have channels ye know not of! Mysterious weapons, mysterious ways, mysterious channels! For God works in mysterious ways His wonders to perform." The trouble with most people is that they want to know the way and the channels beforehand. They want to tell Supreme Intelligence just how their prayers should be answered. They do not trust the wisdom and ingenuity of God. They pray, giving Infinite Intelligence definite directions how to work, thereby limiting the Holy One of Israel.

Pray with the belief that you already have it; have the expectancy of a little child and your prayers will be answered. A child waits with joyful expectancy for his toys at Christmas. I give the illustration of the little boy who asked for a drum for Christmas. The child does not lie awake at night agonizing over his drum wondering whether he will get it. He goes to bed and sleeps like a top. He jumps out of bed in the morning ready for the happy day before him. He looks with wonder at that which is before him.

The grown-up person spends sleepless nights agonizing over his problem. Instead of a drum, he has spoken for a large sum of money. He can't think of any way it can come, and will it come on time? He will tell you he has perfect faith in God, but he would like to know more about the channel and how it is to be done. The answer comes, "I have weapons ye know not of." "My ways are ingenious, my methods are sure."

"Trust in me, commit your ways unto me." Committing your ways unto the Lord seems very difficult to most people. It means, of course, to follow intuition, for intuition is the magic path, the beeline to your demonstration. Intuition is a Spiritual faculty above the intellect. It is the "still small voice" commonly called a hunch, which says, "This is the way, walk ye in it." I refer to intuition very often for it is the most important part of Spiritual development. It is Divine Guidance. It is the God within, it is the eye which watches over Israel and never slumbers or sleeps. With it, nothing is unimportant. Acknowledge me in all your ways and I will make plain your path. Remember —despise not the day of small things (of seemingly unimportant events).

It is very difficult for a person who has always followed the reasoning mind to suddenly follow intuition, especially people who have what they call regular habits. They are accustomed to doing the same thing every day at the same time. Meals like clockwork. They get up at a certain time and go to bed at a certain time. Any deviation upsets them.

We have the power of choice—we may follow the magic path of intuition, or the long and hard road of experience, by following the reasoning mind. By following the superconscious we attain the heights. In the intuition are the pictures of eternal youth and eternal life, where death itself is overcome. We have the power to impress the subconscious mind with the picture of Eternal youth and Eternal life. The subconscious, being simply power without direction, carries out the idea. We see this idea partly expressed in the moving picture "The Lost Horizon." Shangrila was a symbolic picture of the "World of the Wondrous," where all conditions are perfect.

There is a Spiritual prototype of your body and affairs. I call it the Divine Design and this Divine Design is a Perfect Idea in your superconscious mind. Most people are far from expressing the Divine Idea of their bodies and affairs. They have stamped the contrary pictures of disease, old age and death upon the subconscious, and it has carefully carried out their orders. Now we must give a new order; "Let me now express the Divine Idea in my mind, body and affairs." If you will impress the subconscious by repeating this statement you will be amazed at the changes which soon take place. You will be bombarded by new ideas and new ideals. A chemical change will take place in your body. Your environment will change for the better, for you are expanding rapidly into the Divine Plan, where all conditions are permanently perfect.

"Lift up your heads, ye gates, and be ye lifted up, ye everlasting doors; and the King of Glory shall come in. Who is this King of Glory? The Lord (or Law) strong and mighty. The Lord mighty in battle."

Now remember, the Bible is talking about thoughts and states of

159

consciousness. Here is a picture of the Perfect Ideas of the superconscious mind, rushing into your conscious mind. Gates and doors are lifted up, and "The King of Glory comes in."

"Who is this King of Glory? The Lord strong and mighty. The Lord mighty in battle." This King of Glory has weapons ye know not of and puts to flight the army of the aliens (the negative thoughts entrenched in your consciousness for countless ages). These negative thoughts have always defeated the manifestation of your heart's desire. They are the thought forms which you have built up in your subconscious by constantly thinking the same thoughts. You have built up a fixed idea that "Life is hard and filled with disappointments." You will meet these thoughts as concrete experiences in life, for "Out of the imaginations of the heart come the issues of life."

"My ways are ways of pleasantness." We should all build up in consciousness a picture of peace, harmony and beauty and some day it will push itself into visibility. The Divine Idea of your life often flashes across your consciousness as something too good to be true. Very few people fulfill their destinies. Destiny means the place you were destined to fill. We are fully equipped for the Divine Plan of our lives. We are more than equal to every situation. If we could get the realization back of these words doors would fly open and channels be cleared. We could actually hear the hum of Divine activity, for we would be linked with Infinite Intelligence which knows no defeat. Opportunities would come to us from unexpected quarters. Divine activity would operate in and through all our affairs and the Divine Idea would come to pass.

God is Love but God is Law, "If ye love me, keep my commandments" (or laws). Dr. Ernest Wilson told me that his first knowledge of Truth came through reading Emerson's "Concentration." Concentration means loving absorption. We see children lovingly absorbed in their play. We can only be a success in a line which interests us greatly. Great inventors are never bored with their work, or they would not bring forth great inventions. Never try to force a child to be something he does not want to be. He will only prove a failure. The first start toward success is to be glad you are yourself. So many people are bored by themselves.

They have no self-reliance, and are always wishing they were someone else.

When I was in London I saw a man on the street selling a new song, it was called, "I'm tickled to death I'm me." I thought that was a wonderful idea—start out by being glad you are yourself. Then you can expand rapidly into the Divine plan of your life where you fulfill your destiny. You may be sure that the Divine plan of your life will give you perfect satisfaction. You will no longer envy anyone. People often become impatient and discouraged. I was inspired by reading in the paper about Omaha, the famous racehorse. The article said, "Omaha has to run a mile before he gets into his stride." There are, no doubt, a lot of Omahas in the world, but they can get into their Spiritual stride, and win the race, in the twinkling of an eye.

"Delight thyself also in the Lord, and He shall give thee the desires of thine heart." Delight thyself in the law and it will give to thee the desires of thine heart. "Delighting yourself in the law" means to enjoy making a demonstration. To enjoy trusting God means to be happy in following your intuitive leads. Most people say, "Oh dear; I've got to demonstrate money again" or, "Oh dear, my hunches make me so nervous, I haven't the nerve to follow them." People enjoy playing golf and tennis, why can't we enjoy playing the game of life? It is because we are playing with unseen forces. With golf or tennis they have balls they can see and a goal which is visible to the naked eye; but how much more important is this game of life! The goal is the Divine plan of your life where all conditions are permanently perfect.

"In all thy ways acknowledge Him and He will make plain thy paths." Every moment we can link with intuition will give us as definite a lead as a signpost. So many people are leading such complicated lives because they are trying to think things out instead of "intuiting" the way out.

I know a woman who says she has a thorough knowledge of Truth and its application but the minute she has a problem she reasons and weighs and measures the situation. It is never solved. Intuition flies out of the window when reason comes to the door. Intuition is a Spiritual faculty, the superconscious, and never explains itself. There came a voice before me, saying, "This is the way, walk ye in it." Someone asked me if the reasoning mind was ever any good. The reasoning mind must be redeemed. Trust in Spiritual law and "it will be given you."

Your part is to be a good receiver, prepare for your blessing, rejoice and give thanks and it will come to pass.

I have weapons ye know not of, I have ways which will astound you.

Chapter 2 - I GIVE UNTO YOU POWER

God's gift to man is power; power and dominion over all created things; his mind, his body, and affairs. All unhappiness comes from lack of power. Man imagines himself weak and the victim of circumstances, claiming that "Conditions over which he had no control" caused his defeat. Man by himself is indeed a victim of circumstances, but linked with God-power all things are possible.

Through a knowledge of metaphysics we are discovering how this can be done. By your word you contact this power. Then, miraculously, every burden is lifted and every battle is won. Life and death are in the power of the tongue. Watch your words with all diligence. You are continually reaping the fruits of your words. "And he that overcometh and keepeth my works to the end, to him will I give power and dominion over the nations." Overcoming means to conquer all doubts, fears and negative vibrations. One man with perfect peace and perfect poise, filled with love and good-will, could dissolve all negative vibrations. They would melt away like snow under the sun.

This God-power is within you, your superconscious mind. It is the realm of inspiration, revelation and illumination. It is the realm of miracles and wonders. Quick and seemingly impossible changes take place for your good. A door opens where there were no doors. Supply appears from hidden and unexpected channels, for "God has weapons ye know not of."

To work with God-power you must give it right of way and still the reasoning mind. The instant you ask, Infinite Intelligence knows the way of fulfillment. Man's part is to rejoice and give thanks, and act his

Faith. A very well-known woman in England told of this experience: She was asking, with great feeling, for a realization of God. These words came to her "Act as though I were, and I am." It is exactly what I say, over and over again—only active Faith impresses the subconscious, and unless you impress the subconscious, there are no results.

I will now give you an example to show you just how the law works. A woman came to me whose heart's desire was her right marriage and happy home. She was very fond of a certain man, but he was a most difficult person. After having shown her every attention and devotion, he suddenly changed, and dropped out of her life. She was unhappy, resentful and discouraged. I said, "Now this is the time to prepare for your happy home! Buy little things for it as if you hadn't a minute to spare."

She became quite interested in shopping for her happy home, when all appearances were against it. "Now," I said, "you'll have to perfect yourself on the situation and become immune to all resentment and unhappiness." I gave her the statement: "I am now immune to all hurt and resentment; my poise is built upon a rock, the God within." I said, "When you are immune to all hurt and resentment, this man will be given you or his equivalent."

It took many months, when one evening she came to see me and said, "I have only the kindest and most friendly feelings for this man. If he isn't the Divine selection I would be happy without him." Not long after, she happened to meet the man. He was so sorry for the way he had acted. He begged her to forgive him. Not long after, they were married and a happy home came into manifestation. It had built itself around her active Faith.

Your only enemies are within yourself. The woman's enemies were "hurt" and "resentment." They are indeed "serpents and scorpions." Many lives have been wrecked by these two enemies. Linked with God-power, all opposition vanished from this woman's life. Nothing could by any means hurt her.

Think what that means, to have a life free from all unhappy

experiences. It is done through making a conscious contact with God-power every instant.

Many times in the Bible, the word "power" is mentioned. "Thou shalt remember the Lord thy God, for it is He that giveth thee power to get wealth."

A person with a rich consciousness attracts riches. A person with a poor consciousness attracts poverty. I have seen people in this Truth rise out of lack and limitation by linking with the God-power within, not depending on the external. Trusting in God gives you irresistible power, for this Supreme Intelligence only knows the Way of fulfillment. "Trust in Me and I will bring it to pass."

All our knowledge of Truth can bring us is to know that God is the only Power. One Power, one Presence, one Plan.

When you have the fixed idea that there is only one Power in the universe, God-power, all appearance of evil will disappear from your world. In getting a demonstration we must acknowledge only one Power. Evil comes from man's own "vain imaginings." Withdraw all power from evil and it is powerless to hurt.

I will give you an example which shows the working of the law. I was in a restaurant with a friend who spilled something on her dress. She was sure it would leave a stain. I said, "We'll give it a treatment." I made the statement, "Evil is unreal and leaves no stain." I said, "Now, don't look, leave it to Infinite Intelligence." In about an hour we took a look and there was not the slightest stain.

What is true of a little thing is true of a big thing. You can use this statement for past misfortunes or mistakes, and somehow or other, under Grace, the effects will disappear; they will leave no stain.

Many people are using personal-power instead of God-power, which always brings unhappy reaction. Personal-power means forcing personal will. I will give the example of a woman I knew a long time ago. She married a man who worked on a newspaper drawing a comic strip. His drawings demanded a knowledge of slang, which he used on every occasion. She decided he should cultivate his mind and read the classics. They moved to a college town so that he could go to college. She insisted upon his going to college. He resisted a little at first then he grew to like it! Soon he was steeped in the classics. He wouldn't talk anything but Plato and Aristotle. He wanted the food cooked the way they cooked, and eat the simple food they ate. Her life had become a nightmare. After that, she never tried to change people. The only person to change is yourself. As you change, all the conditions around you will change! People will change!

When you are undisturbed by a situation it falls away of its own weight. Your life is outpictured by the sum-total of your subconscious beliefs. Wherever you go, you take these conditions with you.

"I am strong in the Lord and the Power of His might."

"I am backed by unnumbered hosts of power."

Power means dominion and dominion means control. Man controls conditions by a knowledge of Spiritual law. Suppose your problem is lack or limitation. Your urgent need is supply. Link with this God-power within and give thanks for your immediate supply. If you are too close to the situation, if you are filled with doubts and fears, go to a Practitioner for help, someone to see clearly for you.

A man told me while at a Truth Center at Pittsburgh he heard people talking about me and he said, "Who in heck is Florence Scovel Shinn?" Someone replied, "Oh, she wrote The Game of Life, if you write to her she'll get you a miracle." He said he promptly wrote to me and got a demonstration. Do not hesitate to ask for help if you cannot see clearly your good. Of course, you can reach the state where you do not need any help, when you have the fixed idea that God's Power is the only Power and that God's Plan is the only Plan.

We cannot take blessings from Infinite Intelligence; they must be given us. Man's part is to be a grateful receiver.

It isn't until we face a situation of lack that we suddenly express the power which has already been given us. I have known people who are usually nervous and anxious to become poised and powerful when confronted by a big situation. "Hear, Oh Israel! Ye have no need to fight, stand ye still and see the salvation of the Lord." People often ask, "What does it mean to stand still, to do nothing at all?" "Standing still" means to keep your poise. I said to a man who was tense and anxious, "Take it easy and see the salvation of the Lord." He replied, "My, that has helped me a lot." Most people are trying too hard. They carry their burdens and fight their battles and are, therefore, always in a turmoil and never get what we call a demonstration. Stand aside and see the salvation of the Lord. We might paraphrase the Scriptures and say, "Hear! O Israel, you will never win this battle by fighting—leave it entirely to Me, and it will be given you."

Following the magic path of intuition you escape all complications and friction, and make a beeline to your demonstration. Remember we are told not to despise the day of small things. It is a great mistake to think that anything is unimportant. I was going to a shop to buy two articles. In my vicinity are two shops, an expensive one and one where all the things are a little cheaper, but the articles are exactly the same. The reasoning mind said, "Go to the cheaper place" but intuition said, "Go to the expensive place." Of course, I followed that magic path. I told the clerk what I wanted. He said: "The two articles are today sold for the price of one, because they are advertising one of the products."

So intuition led me to the right place and price. The difference in price was only about fifty cents but intuition always looks after our interests. If I had been trying to get something cheap, I would have gone to the other shop and paid twice as much. Learn from the little things, and you will be ready to handle the big things.

Studying closely the Scriptures we find God's gift to man is power. The things and conditions automatically follow. God gives man power to get well. He gives man power over the elements. He gives man power to heal sickness, and to cast out devils.

"They that wait upon the Lord shall renew their strength. They shall mount up with wings and eagles, they shall run and not be weary, and shall walk and not faint."

Let us realize that this invincible power is within reach of all. "Whosoever calleth on the name of the Lord, shall be delivered!" So we find the Word links man with omnipotence. This Supreme Intelligence is more than equal to lifting every burden and fighting every battle.

All power is given unto me to bring my heaven upon my earth.

Chapter 3 - BE STRONG; FEAR NOT

Be strong! Fear not; Fear is man's only adversary. You face defeat whenever you are fearful! Fear of lack! Fear of failure! Fear of loss! Fear of personality! Fear of criticism! Fear robs you of all power, for you have lost your contact with the Universal Power House. "Why are ye fearful, Oh ye of little faith?" Fear is inverted faith. It is faith turned upside down. When you are fearful you begin to attract the thing you fear; you are magnetizing it. You are hypnotized by the race thought when you are afraid.

Daniel was undisturbed because he knew his God was stronger than the lions. His God made the lions as harmless as kittens, so walk up to your lion as quickly as possible and see for yourself. Perhaps all your life you've been running away from some particular lion. It has made your life miserable and your hair grey.

A hairdresser once told me that she knew a woman whose grey hair returned to its natural color when she stopped worry. A woman said to me during an interview, "I'm not a bit fearful, but I worry a lot." Fear and worry are twins and are the same thing. If you were fearless, your worry cells would be dried up. Why are ye worried, Oh ye of little faith? I think the most prevalent fear is the fear of loss. Perhaps you have everything that life can give, but in creeps the old lion of apprehension. You hear him growling, "It's too good to be true! It can't last." If he gets your attention you may well worry.

Many people have lost what they prized most dearly in life. That is because invariably they fear loss. The only weapon you can use against your lions is your word. Your word is your wand, filled with magic and power. You wave your wand over your lion and transmute him into a kitten. But the lion will remain a lion unless you walk up to him. You may well ask, "HOW do we walk up to lions?"

Moses said unto his people, "Fear ye not, stand still and see the salvation of the Lord, which He will show to you this day for the Egyptians whom ye have seen today, ye shall see them again, no more forever! The Lord shall fight for you, and ye shall hold your peace." What a marvelous arrangement!

Infinite Intelligence knows the way out. Infinite Intelligence knows where the supply is for every demand. But we must trust It, keep our poise, and give It right of way. So many people are afraid of other people. They run away from disagreeable situations, so of course, the situation runs after them.

"The Lord is my light and my salvation: whom shall I fear? The Lord is the strength of my life: of whom shall I be afraid?" The twenty-seventh Psalm is one of the most triumphant Psalms! It is also rhythmic and musical. The writer realized that no enemy could harm him, for the Lord was his light and his salvation. Now remember, your only enemies are within yourself. The Bible is speaking of the enemy thoughts - your doubts, fears, hates, resentments, and forebodings. Every negative situation in your life is a crystallized thought; it has been built up out of your own vain imaginings! But these situations cannot stand the light of truth. So, you face the situation fearlessly, saying, "The Lord is my light and salvation; whom shall I fear?"

You must be wiser than your enemy thoughts, the army of the aliens. You must answer every negative thought with a word of authority. The army of the aliens will chant: "Business is dull and money is scarce." Immediately you reply, "My supply comes from God and now appears like mushrooms overnight." There are no hard times in the kingdom. You may have to keep this up for quite a while, but finally you will win out, for the truth must prevail and you have put to flight the army of the aliens. Then, when you are off your guard, the army of the aliens begins again; "You're not appreciated, you'll never be a success." You answer immediately: "God appreciates me, therefore man appreciates me. Nothing can interfere with my divinely designed success."

Finally the army of the aliens is dissolved and dissipated, because you do not give it your attention. You have starved the aliens out. Starve out the fear thoughts by not giving them your attention and acting your

168

faith. The lion draws his fierceness from your fear; his roar is in the tremors of your heart. Stand still like Daniel, and you too shall hear the rush of angels sent to take your part.

Bernard Shaw, in his book Back to Methuselah, says: "Adam invented murder, birth and death and all negative conditions." It was the development of the reasoning mind. Of course, Adam stands for Generic Mind. In the Garden of Eden stage, man functioned only in the superconscious. Whatever he desired or required was always at hand. With the development of the reasoning mind came the fall of man. He reasoned himself into lack, limitations and failure. He earned his bread by the sweat of the brow, instead of being Divinely provided for.

God is the Giver, man the receiver! This Supreme Intelligence supplies man with all that he desires or requires!

A marvelous statement to make to yourself is: "Whereas I was blind, now I can see." Perhaps you were blind to your good, blind to your opportunities, blind to your intuitive leads, blind to appearances, mistaking friends for enemies. When you are awake to your good, you know there are no enemies, for God utilizes every person and situation for your good. Hindrances are friendly and obstacles stepping-stones. One with God, you become invincible.

This is a very powerful statement: "God's Invincible Power sweeps all before it. I ride the waves into my Promised Land." Riding the waves, they take you to your destination, free from the undertow of negative thinking which would pull you down. Your thoughts and desires are always taking you somewhere. Prentice Mulford says: "The persistent purpose, that strong desire, that never ceasing longing, is a seed in the mind. It is rooted there, it is alive! It never stops growing!

There is a wonderful law involved in it. This law when known, followed out and trusted, leads every individual to mighty and beautiful results. The law followed with our eyes open, leads to more and more happiness in life; but followed blindly with our eyes shut, leads to misery!

This means that desire is a tremendous vibratory force and must be rightly directed. Take this statement: "I only desire that which Infinite Intelligence desires through me. I claim that which is mine by Divine right, and under Grace in a Perfect Way!" You will then cease desiring the wrong things, and the right desires will take their place. Your dreary desires are answered drearily, your impatient desires are long delayed or violently fulfilled. It is important never to lose sight of this. Many unhappy situations have been brought about through dreary or impatient desires.

I will give an example of a woman who was married to a man who wanted her to go somewhere with him every evening. It wore her out and night after night she wished impatiently that she could stay at home and read a book. The desire was so strong it commenced to bud. Her husband went off with another woman. She lost him and his support — but she had the time to stay at home and read a book. Nothing has ever come uninvited into your life.

Prentice Mulford has also some interesting ideas on work. He said: "To succeed in any undertaking, any art or any trade or any profession, simply keep it ever persistently fixed in mind as an aim, and then study to make all effort toward it play or recreation. The moment it becomes hard work, we are not advancing."

As I look back on my experiences in the art world, I see how true this is. From the Academy of Fine Arts in Philadelphia came eight men, all of about the same age, who became distinguished and successful artists. They were called "The Eight" in Contemporary Art. Not one of them was ever known to work hard. They never drew from the antique; they never did anything in an academic way. They simply expressed themselves. They painted and drew because they loved it—for the fun of it.

They tell an amusing story of one of them who became a very well-known landscape artist, taking many medals and honorary mentions at exhibits. He had a one-man show in New York City at one of the big galleries, and was seated reading a paper. An enthusiastic woman rushed up to him and said: "Can you tell me anything about the wonderful man who painted these adorable pictures?" He replied:

"Sure, I'm the guy that painted the damn things." He painted for fun, he didn't care whether people liked his pictures or not.

Whereas I was blind, now I can see my right work, my perfect self-expression. Whereas I was blind, now I can see clearly and distinctly the Divine plan of my life. Whereas I was blind, now I can see that God's power is the only power and that God's plan is the only plan. The race thought is still with a belief in insecurity. God is your eternal security of mind, body and affairs. "Let not your heart be troubled, neither be afraid." If you were wide-awake to your good, you could not be troubled and fearful! Waking up to the truth, that there is no loss, lack or failure in the kingdom of reality—loss, lack and failure would disappear from your life. They come from your own vain imaginings.

The following is an example illustrating the working of the law. A number of years ago, when I was in London, I bought a wonderful fountain pen at Asprey's. It was Japanese and was called a Namike Pen. It was quite expensive and they gave me with it a guarantee that it would last thirty years. I was very much impressed because every summer, on the 5th of August, they wrote me asking how the pen was getting along; one might have thought I had bought a horse. It was no ordinary pen and was very satisfactory. I always carried it with me and one day I lost it. I immediately commenced denying loss. I said; "There is no loss in Divine Mind, therefore I cannot lose the Namike Pen. It will be restored to me or its equivalent." No shops that I knew of in New York City carried these pens and London was a long way off, but I was charged with Divine Confidence; I couldn't lose the Namike Pen.

One day, going along Fifth Avenue in a bus, my eye caught a sign on a shop for the fraction of a second. It seemed to stand out in the light. It read, "Oriental Craft Shop." I had never heard of it, but I had a strong hunch to go in and ask for a Namike Pen. I got off the bus and went into the shop and asked. The saleswoman replied, "Why yes, we have quite an assortment — they have just been reduced to $2.50." I praised the Lord and gave thanks. I bought three, and told the above story at one of my meetings. They were soon sold out as people rushed to get them. This was certainly an amazing working of the law — but I was wide-awake to my good. I did not let any grass grow under my intuitive lead.

"Whereas I was blind, now I can see, there is nothing to fear for there is no power to hurt. I see clearly before me the open road of fulfillment. There are no obstacles on my pathway."

Thou madest Him to have dominion over the works of thy hand: thou hast put all things under His feet. --Psalm 8:6

Chapter 4 - THE GLORY OF THE LORD (Psalm 24)

In the dictionary, I find the word 'glory' defined as radiance, splender. "Mine eyes have seen the radiance of the Lord", that means the law in action. We cannot see God, for God is Principle, Power, the Supreme Intelligence within us; but what we see are the proofs of God. "Prove Thou me herewith, saith the Lord of Hosts, if I will not open the windows of hearing, and pour you out a blessing, so great, there be not room enough to receive it." We prove God by directing God-power and trusting in It to do the work. Every time we get a demonstration we have proved God. If you have not received the desires of the heart, you have "asked amiss," that is, you have "not prayed aright." You receive your answer in the same way in which you sent out your demand. Your dreary desires are answered drearily, your impatient desires are long delayed or violently fulfilled.

Suppose you are resenting lack and limitation and living in poor surroundings. You say with great feeling, "I want to live in a big house, with beautiful surroundings!" Sooner or later, you may find yourself a caretaker in a big and beautiful house, but you have no share in this opulence. This idea came to me as I was passing Andrew Carnegie's house and grounds on Fifth Avenue. It was all closed and the entrance and windows boarded up. There was just one window open in the basement. This is where the caretaker lived. It was certainly a dreary picture. So ask (or wish) with praise and thanksgiving, so that you will see the glory of the law in action.

All life is vibration. You combine with what you notice, or you combine with what you vibrate to. If you are vibrating to injustice and resentment you will meet it on your pathway, at every step. You will certainly think it is a hard world and that everybody is against you. Hermes Trismegistus said several thousand years ago, "To change your mood you must change your vibrations." I make it even stronger; I say, to change your world, you must change your vibrations. Turn on a different current in your battery of thought, and you'll see the difference immediately. Suppose you have been resenting people and saying you are not appreciated. Take the statement: "God appreciates me, therefore, man appreciates me, I appreciate myself." Immediately you will meet with some recognition on the external.

You are now a master workman and your tools are your words. Be sure you are building constructively, according to the Divine Plan.

We are now coming into an understanding age. We no longer have the faith of peasants, we have understanding faith. Solomon said: "With all your getting, get understanding"; understanding of the working of Spiritual Law, so that we distribute this power within us in a constructive way.

The law of laws is to do unto others as you would be done by; for, whatever you send out comes back and what you do to others will be done to you. So, the woman who refrains from criticizing, saves herself from criticism. Critical people are always being criticized. They are living in that vibration. They also have rheumatism, for acid thoughts produce acid in the blood, which causes pain in the joints.

I read an article in the newspaper. It said a physician had had a peculiar experience with one of his patients. The woman had boils every time her mother-in-law paid her a visit. There is nothing peculiar in this, as she was boiling within (how many times we have heard people say they were in a boiling rage), so the boils appeared on her body. This does not include all mothers-in-law. I have known some very wonderful ones who have brought only peace and harmony with them.

Skin trouble shows that someone has got under your skin. You have been irritated or angered. Here we see again that man gives direction to this God-power, through himself. Vibrative to this power, all things are under his feet. "All sheep and oxen, yea the beasts of the field. The fowl of the air and the fish of the sea, whatsoever passes through the paths of the seas." What a picture of power and dominion for man!

Man has power and dominion over the elements. We should be able "to rebuke the wind and the waves." We should be able to put an end to drought. I read in the paper that the people in a certain drought district were requested not to sing, "It ain't going to rain no more." Knowing something of metaphysics, they realized the power of negative words. They felt it had something to do with the drought. We should be able to stop floods and epidemics, "For man is given power and dominion over all created things." Every time we get a demonstration we are proving our power and dominion.

We must be lifted up in consciousness for the King of Glory to come in! As we read the statement: "If thine eye be single, thy whole body shall be full of light," we seem flooded with an inner radiance. The single eye means to see good only, to be undisturbed by appearances of evil. The imaging faculty is a creative faculty, and your fear-pictures will appear on the external, the result of your own distorted imagination. With the single eye, man sees only the Truth. He sees through evil, knowing out of it comes good. He transmutes injustice into justice and disarms his seeming enemies by sending good will. He is now backed by unnumbered hosts of Power, for the single eye sees only victory.

We read in mythology of the Cyclops, a race of giants said to have inhabited Sicily. These giants had only one eye in the middle of the forehead. The seat of the imaging faculty is situated in the forehead (between the eyes), so these fabled giants came from this idea. You are, indeed, a giant, when you have "the single eye."

"TODAY is the day of your salvation." A few days ago, I saw a motion picture which showed the futility of trying to live in or bring back the past. It is a French picture and is called "Life Dances On." It is the story of a woman, who, when sixteen, had gone to her first ball. She is now a widow of about thirty-five. She had married for money and had never known happiness. When burning old papers, she came across a faded dance program. On it were the names of six men she had danced with at the ball. Each had sworn to love her all his life! As she sits with the program in her hands the memory of the ball is pictured on the screen; a scene of loveliness, the dancers almost floating to the strains of an entrancing waltz. Her life is now empty and she decides to recover her lost youth, by finding out what had become of the men whose names were on the program. A friend who is with her says, "You cannot re-capture your lost youth; if you go back you lose the things of today."

However, she goes in search of them, and with all comes disillusion. One did not remember her at all. When she said: "Don't you remember me? I am Christine!" He replied, "Christine who?" Some of them were living sordid lives. At last she returns to the town of her girlhood, where the fifth man lived. He had become a hairdresser. He talks to her gaily of old times while he gives her a permanent wave. He says, "I don't suppose you remember your first ball, it was right here in this town, and tonight there will be a dance in the same place. Do come with me, it will remind you of the old days!"

She goes to the ball; everything looks cheap and tawdry. Unattractive, badly dressed people are on the dance floor. She requests the orchestra to play her waltz, the waltz of her lost youth! Her escort tells her the others won't like such an old-fashioned waltz. However, they play it. The contrast is too much; all her illusions have vanished. She realizes the ball she remembers never really existed the way she thought it did. It was only an illusion of the past. She could not re-capture her past.

Most people's lives are a succession of disturbances: lack, loss, limitation, mothers-in-law, landlords, debt or injustice. This world was popularly known as a "vale of tears." People were all mixed up in their own affairs, fighting their battles and carrying their burdens. If a man judges by appearances, he finds himself in an arena most of the time. The arena of adverse conditions and facing lions of lack and limitation. "If thine eye be evil (if you are imaging adverse conditions) thy whole body shall be full of darkness. If, therefore, the light that is in thee be darkness, how great is that darkness!" The light of the body is the inner eye (or imaging faculty); if, therefore, thine eye be single, you are seeing only one power, one plan and one planner, your body and affairs will be full of Light. See yourself, daily, bathed in the Light of God.

This inner radiance is invincible power and dissolves anything not Divinely planned. It dissolves all appearance of disease, lack, loss or limitation. It dissolves adverse conditions, or "any weapon that is formed against you."

We have always at our command this Light, when your eye is single. We should learn to turn on this Light with the same assurance with which we turn on the electric light. "Seek ye first the kingdom of God and His righteousness and all right things shall be added unto you." The Chinese Proverb says: "The philosopher leaves the cuff of his coat to the tailor." So, leave the plan of your life to the Divine Planner and you will find all conditions permanently perfect.

Chapter 5 - PEACE AND PROSPERITY

"Peace be within thy walls and Prosperity within thy Palaces." In this statement from the 122nd Psalm we find that peace and prosperity go hand in hand. People who are manifesting the appearance of lack are in a state of fear and confusion. They are not wide-awake to their good and miss leads and opportunities. A peaceful person is a wide-awake person. He sees clearly and acts quickly. He never misses a trick.

I have seen people discordant and unhappy changed completely. I will give an example in order to prove the working of the law. A woman came to me in a state of abject sorrow. She looked the part. Her eyes were blurred from constant weeping. Her face was haggard and drawn. The man she loved had left her and she was certainly the most demagnetized creature I had ever seen. I noticed the shape of her face - large eyes, far apart and a pointed chin. For many years I was an artist and have got into the habit of looking at people from an artist's standpoint. As I looked at this forlorn creature, I thought, her face has the modeling of a Botticelli. I often see Rembrandts, Sir Joshua Reynolds, etc., in people I meet.

I spoke the Word for this woman and gave her my book, The Game of Life and How to Play it. A week or two afterwards, in walked a very dashing person. Her eyes were beautiful and she was very pretty. I thought, her face has the modeling of a Botticelli. Suddenly I realized it was the same woman! She was happy and carefree! What had happened? Our talk and the book had brought her peace.

"Peace be within your walls!" Your "walls" are your consciousness. Peace and rest exist in your superconscious mind, in the God within, where there are no burdens and no battles. The doubts and fears and negative pictures are in the subconscious. When I was returning from California some years ago, I came in an airplane. In the high altitudes I had a queer detached feeling. In that high altitude we are at peace with ourselves and with the whole world. In the high altitudes the fields are always white with the harvest. Only the emotions keep you from reaping your harvest of success, happiness and abundance. People are rocked with doubts and fears, bringing failure, unhappiness and disease.

I read in a daily paper that the laws of the mind are being generally recognized and understood. It has been found that the fear of failure is the greatest of all fears, and at least seventy-five percent of those examined psychologically have this failure fear. Of course, this may refer to failure of health, failure in business, finances, love, success, etc. Other important fears are fear of the dark, fear of being alone, fear of animals. Some people fear they will be misunderstood, while others fear they are losing mental control. Constant and continued fear affects the glands—interferes with digestion and is usually associated with distressing nervous symptoms. It robs the body of health and destroys happiness.

Fear is man's worst enemy, for you attract what you fear. It is Faith turned upside down. It is really Faith in evil instead of good. "Why are ye fearful Oh! Ye of little faith?" The fearless, unfettered mind attracts to itself all good. Whatever you desire or require is already on your pathway. "Before ye call I have answered."

Suppose we paraphrase the Scriptures and say: "Whatever you desire or require is already planted on your pathway." Often a new word will give you sudden realization. If you are in need of any information, it will be given you. A friend told me of this surprising working of the law. She was translating an old Italian manuscript on the life of an early

177

Persian ruler. No books in English had been written on the subject. She wondered why the publishers were holding back its publication. One evening she was eating her dinner at the Automat. She fell into a conversation with a man at the same table. She told him of the work she was doing and of the translation of the early Italian manuscript. He suddenly volunteered the information; "You'll have a hard time getting it published because this Persian ruler's ideas conflict with the ideas of the present government." He was a student and scholar and knew more than she did on the subject.

Her question was answered and at the Automat. Such information could, usually, be gleaned only in the archives of some public library. God works in unexpected places His wonders to perform. She had worried about it, but when she was peaceful and happy and unconcerned, the information sailed in over a calm sea.

"Our feet shall stand within thy gates, O Jerusalem." Jerusalem stands for peace and the feet for understanding. So understanding always brings us within the gates of peace. How can a person attain peace when his whole life is in a turmoil? By taking an affirmation. You cannot control your thought but you can control your words, and eventually the word wins out. Most people have attracted inharmonious conditions because they have been fighting their battles and carrying their burdens. We must learn to get out of God's way so that He can harmonize or adjust the situation

The word "harmonize" is a very good one, for I have seen crooked places made straight, and adjustments made, that no human mind could have thought of. All that the Kingdom affords is yours if you will give Infinite Intelligence right of way, for it has already supplied a lavish supply for every demand. But It must be fully trusted. If you doubt or fear, you lose your contact with this Supreme Force. So if you are filled with doubts and fears, it is necessary to do something to show your faith. "Faith without works (or action) is dead." Active Faith impresses the subconscious with expectance and you keep your contact with Universal Intelligence. Just as Wall Street watches the market, we must watch our Faith market. Often the Faith market is down. Sometimes it goes down and down until a crash comes: some unhappy situation which we could have prevented. We realize we followed reason instead of intuition.

A woman told me how she had several definite leads not to follow a certain course. In spite of this she followed the reasoning mind and great unhappiness developed from it. Intuition is our unerring guide. Practice following it in little things, then you will trust it in big things. I have a friend who is very intuitive. She sometimes calls up and says: "I've just had a hunch to call you up so I thought I would find out what it is about." Invariably I have some mission for her.

We are indeed living magic lives—guided, protected and provided for. All fear would be banished forever with a realization of this amazing system the Universal has provided for man. He would be unmoved by adverse appearances, knowing as the early Hebrews knew, "that God goes before and every battle is won."

A friend told me a very interesting story. A man in the paper business in Kalamazoo, Michigan, has given away a thousand of my books to his employees. He went into business on a small capital and gave up cold judgment and reasoning. He has built up a twelve million dollar business by following leads and hunches. All his workers have a knowledge of metaphysical law.

Another man who built his business upon the law of giving and receiving met with the same amazing success. He came to Philadelphia with a little money and bought a magazine, an old publication. His desire was to give the people a great deal for a very small price. He believed in the law of giving. It proved to be one of the most popular magazines. He gave the public the best in the way of stories and illustrations and paid well for them. The more he gave, the more he received—millions poured in!! "Peace be within thy walls and prosperity within thy palaces!" Peace and prosperity go hand in hand. "Great peace have they that love Thy law and nothing shall offend them." This law is the law of non-resistance. "Resist not evil, overcome evil with good." Transmute all failure into success, lack into plenty, and discord into peace.

179

Chapter 6 - YOUR BIG OPPORTUNITY

You have only one judge—your word.

Every day is a day of Judgment. We used to be taught that it would be at the end of the world. Look back in your life and see how you have attracted either happiness or disaster through your words. The subconscious has no sense of humor. People joke destructively about themselves and the subconscious takes it seriously. It is because the mental picture you make while speaking impresses the subconscious and works out on the external. A person who knows the power of the word becomes very careful of his conversation. He has only to watch the reaction of his words to know they do not return void. People make their worst mistakes by speaking while they are angry or resentful, because there is so much ill-feeling back of their words. Owing to the vibratory power of words, what you voice, you begin to attract. People who continually speak of disease invariably attract disease.

Invisible forces are ever working for man who is always pulling the strings himself, though he does not know it. We read in the Bible, "Life and death are in the power of the tongue." Yet most people are speaking destructively from morning until night. It is because they have formed a habit of criticism, condemnation and complaint and are eager to tell you of their misfortunes and how mean all their relatives are. They wear their friends out and people avoid them. They are talking themselves into a flock of troubles. Now that we know the power of the word, why not take advantage of it? We take advantage of the radio, the telephone and airplanes, but live with the Mound-builders in conversation.

Science and religion are now coming together. Science is discovering the power within the atom; metaphysics teaches the power within thoughts and words. We are dealing with dynamite when we deal with words. Think of the power of the word in healing! A word is spoken and a chemical change takes place in the body.

One of my friends was seriously ill. The doctor said she had chronic bronchitis and was on the verge of pneumonia. Her daughters and the doctor rushed her to bed and she had a nurse, but weeks passed and there was no improvement. She was a Truth student but for over a year had attended no meetings nor had she kept up her reading. One morning she telephoned me and said, "Please speak the word and get me out of this! I can't stand it any more; I'm not sick, I'm just disgusted. So much negative talk and thought have almost floored me."

Through the spoken word and her affirmation of Truth immediately there was a change for the better. She had a strong hunch to go out and was told it would be dangerous, but by this time she was following Divine Guidance. She went out and called on me and said she was going to attend a luncheon the next day. What had happened? The words of Truth were making a change in her mind and a chemical change was taking place in her body. We are told that if we believe, never doubting, we can say to that mountain, "Be thou removed," and it would disappear into the sea.

The inexhaustible energy in man is released by good-will. A man free from fear, undisturbed by appearances, sending good-will to men and nations, could say to these mountains of hate and war; "Be thou removed" and they would return to their native nothingness.

Resentment and intolerance rob man of his power. We should have signs in the subways and shops: "Watch your thoughts!" "Watch your words!"

Let us now be careful in directing this dynamic force within us. Let us direct it to heal, bless and prosper and direct it in waves of good to the whole world. It goes out a mighty force, but noiseless! Thought, the strongest power in the Universe is without sound. Your good-will sweeps all obstacles from your pathway and your heart's desire is released for you.

What is really yours? The answer is: "All that the kingdom affords is yours." Every righteous desire of the heart is promised you. There are three thousand promises in the Bible, but these gifts can come to us only if we can believe them possible, for everything comes through you —not to you. All life is vibration. Feel rich, and you attract riches. Feel successful and you become successful.

I knew of a small boy who was born in a little country town with no advantages, but he always felt successful; he had the conviction that when he grew up he would be a big artist. No one could discourage him because he was success; he had only success thoughts; he radiated success. At an early age he left the small town and went to a big city and to support himself. He got a position as a newspaper artist on a daily paper, all this without previous preparation. It never occurred to him that it could not be done. He went to an art school and immediately became a shining light. He never studied in an academic way. Whatever he once saw he remembered. In a few years he went to a still larger city and became a well-known artist. This success came to him because he was always seeing success. "I will give to you the land that thou seeth."

The children of Israel were told that they could have all the land that they could see. The Bible is a metaphysical book and it is speaking to the individual. This minute, it says to each one of us, "I will give to you the land that thou seeth." So, what are you seeing with your inner eye? What pictures are you inviting into your life? The imaging faculty has been called the scissors of the mind. If you have failure thoughts, reverse the thought with a success thought. This sounds easy enough to do, but when a failure thought has become a habit, it takes eternal vigilance to dislodge it. That is when a powerful affirmation is needed. You cannot always control your thought but you can control your word, and eventually the word impresses the subconscious and wins out. If you are in a negative state of mind just take the statement: "I look with wonder at that which is before me!" It creates an expectancy of something wonderful and something wonderful will come to you. Cultivate the feeling that miracles and wonders are coming to pass. Cultivate a success expectancy.

Very few people bring into life what is rightfully theirs. They live on the outskirts of their heart's desire. It always seems too good to be true. To the person spiritually awake nothing is too good to be true.

If you want to hear people talking who are still asleep in the Adamic dream, go to a hairdresser's establishment. The Adamic dream is the illusion of opposites. Adam fell into a deep sleep, having eaten of the tree of illusion. Of course, Adam stands for generic man—the race-man. The race-man vainly imagined loss, lack, failure, sin, sickness and death. The awakened man knows only one power, God, and one condition, good. But now we will return to the beauty parlor. The following is an exact quotation and a good example of what one hears:

A woman sat down near me and said in a loud voice, "This place is too warm! Turn something on or open something." The attendant said to her, "How are you feeling today, Mrs. S?" She replied with a heavy sigh, "Oh, I'm pretty well, but I have a hard time keeping well." To the manicurist she said, "Why don't you wear glasses?" The girl replied, "I don't need glasses, why should I wear them?" The woman replied, "Because everybody wears them. You'll find there is something wrong with your eyes if you have them examined." When she finally leaves they all feel limp and wonder if they are really well or only seem to be well. She leaves a trail of apprehension and gloom. This is a sample of what one hears from nearly every booth; the way most people talk. It is appalling when one knows the power of the word and what they are attracting, for they are nearly all describing illnesses or operations.

You combine with what you notice so do not describe anything destructive for you begin to combine with it.

What is really yours? The blessings you bring to yourself, through your spoken or silent word; the things you see with your inner eye. Only your doubts, fears and resentments keep your good from you. If you hate or resent a situation, you have fastened it to you, for you attract what you fear or dislike. For example: someone has been unjust to you and you are filled with wrath and resentment. You cannot forgive that person. Time rolls on and another person does the same thing. It is because you have a picture of injustice engraved in your subconscious. History will repeat itself until you think you are cursed with misfortune and injustice.

There is only one way to neutralize it. Be absolutely undisturbed by injustice and send good-will to all concerned. "My good-will is a strong tower round about me. I now transmute all enemies into friends, all inharmony into harmony, all injustice into justice." You will be amazed at the working of the law. One student brought harmony out of chaos in her business affairs by that statement.

Do not look back and hash over hard times, or you will be drawn back into these conditions. Give thanks for the dawn of a new day. You must be immune to all discouragement and adverse appearances.

All that you desire or require is already on your pathway, but you must be wide awake to your good to bring it into manifestation. After making statements of Truth you suddenly have a flash of realization. You suddenly feel yourself in a new environment. You feel old negative conditions falling away. I once said to a woman, "The walls of lack and delay now crumble away, and you enter your promised land, under grace." She said she had a sudden flash of a wall crumbling away and that she stepped over it. Soon after that, the change came, and she really did enter her Promised Land of Plenty.

I knew a woman whose daughter's desire was a home and husband. In her early youth she had had a broken engagement. Whenever a possible marriage appeared on the horizon, she became frantic with fear and apprehension, picturing vividly another disappointment, and she had several. Her mother came to me to speak the word for her right marriage, Divinely designed, which could not be interfered with. During the interview the mother said continually: "Poor Nellie! Poor Nellie!"

I said: "Do not call your daughter 'poor Nellie' again. You are helping her to be demagnetized. Call her 'Lucky Nellie,' 'Fortunate Nellie,' for you must have faith that God now gives to her the desires of her heart." The mother and daughter persisted in making their affirmations. She has now fulfilled her destiny for she is Mrs. Nellie, the demon of fear dissolved forever.

There are wonderful statements in the Bible referring to the breaking down of negative thought-forms. "The power of the Spirit is mighty even unto the pulling down of strongholds". The human mind is helpless to cope with these negative thoughts. The victory is won by the God within, the superconscious mind.

Chapter 7 - IN NOTHING BE ANXIOUS

All through the Bible we are told not to be anxious, not to be fearful, not to hoard or save, because an invincible, invisible power is at man's command to supply every need. But we were told that it would not work unless we believed in it. "If thou canst believe in this God Power, all things are then possible." It is difficult for man to believe in this power because he has had a right training in unbelief. "I'll believe only what I can see," was supposed to be the height of wisdom. We lived in a world of externals, where we thought everything "just happened." We did not know that back of every happening was a cause, that we, ourselves, started in motion the machinery which produced good or evil in our pathway.

We did not know that words and thoughts are a form of dynamite, and should be handled carefully, with wisdom and understanding. We hurled out into the ethers words of anger, resentment or self-pity, then wondered why life was so hard.

Why not experiment with faith; trust this invisible God-Power and "In nothing be anxious," but "In everything by prayer and thanksgiving, let your requests be made known unto God." Could anything be more simple or direct? Anxiety and habit have become habits. The old thought-forms you have built up in the subconscious hang on like barnacles on an ocean liner. But the ocean liner is put in dry-dock once in a while to have the barnacles scraped off, so, your mental barnacles will have to go through the same process. The dry-dock is a big situation.

I know of a woman who had been a coward all her life, particularly about finances. She worried all the time about money. She came into this Truth, realized how she had limited herself, and suddenly made the giant swing into faith. She commenced to trust God and not the external for her supply. She followed her intuitive leads about spending. If any of her clothes made her feel poor, she would discard them at once, getting something new to make her feel rich. She had very little money, but gave one-tenth (a tithe) to good works. She was winding herself up into a new vibration. Very soon, things commenced to change on the external. A woman on whom she had no claim, who was merely an old friend of her family, left her a thousand dollars. A few months later, another thousand came in. Then a big door opened for her supply and many thousands came in. She had tapped her invisible supply from the Bank of the Universal. She had looked to God only for her supply, then the channels opened. The point I am bringing out is, that she had lost all anxiety about money matters. She had established in her subconscious the firm conviction that her supply came from God, and it never failed.

Man is an instrument for Infinite Intelligence to work through. It will express through him as success, happiness, abundance, health and perfect self-expression, unless fear and anxiety make a short-circuit. If we want examples of fearless faith, go to the circus! The circus people perform seemingly impossible feats because they think they can, and see themselves doing it. Faith means that you can see yourself receiving all these things that you desire. "I will give to thee the land that thou seest."

You can never do a thing you cannot see yourself doing, or fill a place you cannot see yourself filling—not visualizing, making a mental picture (this is a mental process and often brings wrong and limited results); it must be a spiritual realization, a feeling that you are already there; be in its vibration.

I was very much impressed with the story of a great football player who was the greatest all-round athlete in the world, who trained in a hammock. One day he was lying there drowsing in the sun and the trainer came up to him with tears streaming down his face and said; "Jim, for the love of Mike and your country, won't you get up and out of that hammock and do something?" Jim opened one eye and said; "I was just thinking about that. I was going to send for you." "Good," said the trainer. "What do you want me to do?" "First," said Jim, "I want you to mark off twenty-five feet there on the ground." The trainer did so. "Then what?" said the trainer. "That's all," said Jim, and he closed his eyes and swung happily. After at least five minutes he opened them and looked at the marks for a few seconds and then closed his eyes again. "What's the idea?" yelled the trainer. "What are you doing?" Jim looked at him reproachfully and replied: "I'm practicing the broad jump." He did all his training in a hammock: seeing himself doing the broad jump.

Without the vision my people perish, in lack and limitation. You may work very hard on the external and accomplish nothing, if you are without vision. Vision means to see clearly where you are going. To keep your eye on the goal. All men who have accomplished big things have done this.

James J. Hill, who built the Great Northern Railroad, said before a rail was laid, he heard with his inner ear the rumble of the trains and whistle of the engines. He had many obstacles to overcome, but his vision was so clear, it possessed him. One thing in his favor was that his wife believed in him. It is said that it takes two to make a dream come true.

Henry Ford, speaking of his mother-in-law said she was a fine woman, "She believed in me."

"When two of you agree, it shall be done." If you believe in yourself, others will believe in you. As you believe in yourself and the God-power within, fear and anxiety drop away. You establish the vibration of assurance. This is true of an intuitive person. Every move is made under Divine guidance and he never violates a "hunch," therefore he is always in his right place at the right time. However, it often takes great courage to follow intuition. It takes a Viking who is unafraid to sail in unknown seas. Claude Bragdon says: "To live intuitively is to live fourth-dimensionally." The magic path leads you out of the land of Egypt, out of the house of bondage. It is invaluable in business.

Never submit a hunch to someone on the reasoning plane. Those who have ears to hear, let them hear their intuitive leads, and give instant obedience.

"Whatsoever thou wilt ask of God, God will give it thee." This is true of each one. But if we have not received all the blessings of life, we have neglected to ask, or have not "asked aright." The Bible is teaching spiritual law and we must study and use it from every angle in order to set the great machinery of asking and receiving in motion. Every machine must be greased and oiled to be kept in good working order. Active faith and expectancy keep the machine of asking and receiving in perfect order. The following are some of the lubricants which keep it working. "When ye pray, believe ye have it." "In nothing be anxious." "Stand ye still and see the salvation of the Lord." "Do not limit the Holy One of Israel." Realization is manifestation.

Pray with praise and thanksgiving. Some people pray filled with anger and resentment. A woman wrote to me the other day saying: "I have just had a good talk with God and I told Him just what He ought to do about it." She was in the habit of ordering people around and looked upon God as someone she could bully into doing something for her. God is the Supreme Intelligence within each one of us and we are the channels for It to express Itself. We must be non-resistant, poised and peaceful, expecting our good to come to pass. We are the receivers, God is the Giver, and He must create His own channels. We find there is quite an art in praying aright. God must have right of way; His way, not your way. The moment you make your demand Infinite Intelligence knows the way of fulfillment. If you decide how your prayer shall be answered, you have blocked the divinely designed channel. Then you are apt to say: "I never have my prayers answered." We must acquire a technique and send out a sincere desire, which is a prayer. We are free from all clutch or anxiety when we say: "If this is according to the divine plan, we will receive it, if not, give us its equivalent." Be careful not to force anything not divinely planned.

We must know that linked with God-power, nothing can defeat us. "God's ways are ingenious, His methods are sure."

Two of the most beautiful Psalms are the twenty-third and the one hundred and twenty-first. Both give one a feeling of absolute security and were written by a man who had experienced the working of spiritual law.

The God within protects, guides and provides when fully trusted. Most people lose what they love most through fear of loss; they take every precaution on the external, not trusting the protection to the "Eye which watches over Israel." Put whatever you love under the law of divine protection.

The most important part of demonstrating is showing fearless faith. "I will go before thee and make the crooked places straight! I will break in pieces the gates of brass and cut in sunder the bars of iron." The Bible is talking about states of consciousness. "The gates of brass" and "bars of iron," are your doubts, fears, resentments and anxieties. The gates of brass and bars of iron are of our own making and come from our own vain imaginings, a belief in evil.

There is a story of a herd of wild elephants: they were corralled in an enclosure but the men had no way of keeping them in, so they dug stakes and put a rope all around the enclosure. The elephants thought they could not get out. They could have just walked over the rope and stepped out but they had the illusion that the rope kept them in. This is the way with people: doubt and fear is a rope stretched around their consciousness. It makes it impossible for them to walk out into clear thinking.

Clear vision is like a man with a compass; he knows where he is going. Let intuition be your compass and it will always get you out of the woods. Even a man without a compass, led by intuition, would find his way out of the jungle, or be able to steer a ship at sea. Intuition will tell you to walk over the rope. It is amazing how people have overlooked their most important faculty—intuition. Always on man's pathway is his message or lead. Often our leads seem trivial and silly. A person purely on the intellectual plane would dismiss them at once, but the Truth student always has his spiritual ear to the spiritual ground, knowing he is receiving orders from the Infinite. The Bible speaks often of "the still small voice." It is a voice which is not an actual voice, though sometimes actual words are registered on the inner ear.

When we ask for guidance and lay aside the reasoning mind we are tapping the Universal supply of all knowledge; anything necessary for you to know will be revealed to you. Some people are naturally intuitive and are always in contact with Universal Intelligence, but by taking an affirmation we make a conscious contact. Prayer is telephoning to God, and intuition is God telephoning to you. Many people have a "busy wire" when God telephones and they don't get the message. Your wire is "busy" when you are discouraged, angry or resentful. You've heard the expression "I was so mad I couldn't see straight." We might add, "I was so mad I couldn't hear straight." Your negative emotions drown out the voice of intuition.

When you are discouraged, angry, or resentful, is the time to make a statement of Truth, in order to get out of the woods of despair and limitation, for "Whosoever calleth on the name of the Lord shall be delivered!" There is a way out—"Reveal to me the way."

We must stop planning, plotting and scheming and let Infinite Intelligence solve the problem in Its own way. God power is subtle, silent and irresistible. It levels mountains and fills in valleys and knows no defeat! Our part is to prepare for our blessings and follow our intuitive leads.

We now give Infinite Intelligence right-of-way.

Chapter 8 - FEARLESSNESS

All through the Bible man is told not to be afraid. Fear is man's only enemy. It is faith turned upside-down. If you can only believe, all things are possible. Linked with God-power, man is invincible.

The story of Jehosophat is the story of the individual. So often he seems outnumbered by adverse appearances but he hears the same voice of the Infinite saying: "Be not afraid or dismayed by reason of this great multitude, for the battle is not yours but God's." Jehosophat and his army were even told that they would not need to fight the battle. "Set yourselves, stand ye still and see the salvation of the Lord," for the battle was God's not theirs. Jehosophat appointed singers unto the Lord to praise the beauty of holiness as they went out before the army, saying; "Praise the Lord for His mercy endureth forever." When they came toward the watchtower in the wilderness they looked toward the multitude and behold, they were dead. The enemy had destroyed itself. There was nothing to fight.

The Bible is talking about states of consciousness. Your enemies are your doubts and fears, your criticisms and your resentments. Every negative thought is an enemy. You may be outnumbered by adverse appearances, but be not afraid or dismayed by reason of this great multitude; for the battle is not yours but God's.

As we follow closely the story of Jehosophat, we see he advanced making an affirmation: "Praise the Lord, His mercy endureth forever." He had nothing to say about the enemy or his own lack of strength. He was giving the Lord his full attention, and when he commenced to sing and praise, the Lord placed ambushments against his enemies and they were smitten. When you make your statements of Truth, your enemy thoughts are vanquished, dissolved and dissipated, therefore all adverse appearances disappear. When Jehosophat and his army came toward the watchtower in the wilderness, they looked into the multitude and behold they were dead. The watchtower in the wilderness is your high state of consciousness, your fearless faith, your place of safety. There you rise above all adverse conditions, and God's battle is won.

"When Jehosophat and his people came to take away the spoils of the enemy, they found among them both riches and precious jewels, more than they could carry away, and they were three days in gathering of the spoil, it was so much." That means, when you let God fight the battle for you, great blessings come out of every adverse situation. "For thy God will turn the curse into a blessing, for the Lord thy God loveth thee." The ingenuity of the Spirit is amazing. It is pure intelligence and brooks no interference with its plans. It is very difficult for the average person to "stand still," which means, keep your poise, and let Infinite Intelligence run the situation. People like to rush into the battle and try to manage things themselves, which brings defeat and failure.

"Ye shall not need to fight in this battle; set yourselves, stand ye still and see the salvation of the Lord with you. Tomorrow go out against them, for the Lord will be with you." That means, not to run away from the situation, walk up fearlessly and face the lion on your pathway, and the lion turns into an airedale. The lion takes his fierceness from your fear. A great poet has said "Courage has genius, magic and power in it."

Daniel was unafraid and the lions' mouths were closed. King Darius called to Daniel while he was yet in the lions' den, asking him if God could save him from the lions, and Daniel answered, "O! King live forever! My God hath sent His angels and shut the lions' mouths that they have not hurt me." We have in this story the subdued attitude of the lions as a result of Spiritual power; the entire group changed from ferocity to docility, and Daniel looking away from the beasts to the Light and Might of Spirit, which saved him completely from the lions. Scarcely a day passes without some sort of lion appearing on man's pathway, the lions of lack, limitation, fear, injustice, dread or forebodings. Immediately walk up to the situation of which you are afraid. If you run away from it, it will always be right at your heels.

Many people lose the things they prize or love because they are continually fearing their loss. They do everything possible on the external to insure protection, but back of it all is the devastating picture of fear. In order to hold the things you prize and love, you must know that they are Divinely protected, therefore, nothing can harm them.

I give the example of a woman who was very fond of a man who was good-looking and popular with women. She decided to prevent his meeting one particular woman of her acquaintance because she was sure the woman would make every effort to "cut her out," to use a slang expression. One evening she went to the theater and there he was with the woman. They had met at a card party. Her fears had actually attracted the situation. I knew a woman who had seven children. She knew they were all Divinely protected and they all grew up safe and sound. One day a neighbor rushed in and said, "You had better call your children, they are all climbing up and down trees—they are going to kill themselves!" My friend replied, "O they're only playing tree-tag. Don't look at them and nothing will happen." Like Daniel she turned her back to the situation and let God take care of it.

The average person is a resenter, a resister, or a regretter. They resent people they know and people they don't know. They resist everything from daylight saving up. They regret what they did or what they didn't do. It is very wearing to be with these people. They exhaust all their friends. It is because they are not living in the wonderful NOW and are losing all the tricks in the game of life.

It is heaven to be unafraid and to live fully in the NOW; that is, to be fearless in using what we have, knowing back of us is the abundance of the spheres to draw upon. We know that fearless faith and the spoken word release this supply. The power of the word was known in Egypt thousands of years ago.

We read in the Bible, "Behold I make all things new!" By our words of Truth we can make new our minds, bodies and affairs. When all fear is obliterated we live magic lives. Like Jehosophat we go forward fearlessly singing: "Praise the Lord, His mercy endureth forever." In our watch-tower of high consciousness, we stand still and see the salvation of the Lord.

Religion is founded on faith. Faith gives one a sublime assurance of one's good. One may be surrounded by adverse appearances, but this sublime assurance impresses the subconscious mind, and a way opens for the manifestation of health, wealth and happiness. There is an endless, invisible supply for every man.

At the World's Fair there was a panorama of New York City in the Edison Building. At dusk when the city was being lighted up, the buildings showed a myriad of lights; the man explaining the exhibit said: "The city is lighted by the power of electricity at the turn of a switch—the turn of a hand." Edison was the man who had faith in the laws of electricity. He knew what could be done with it if it were harnessed and directed. It seemed to have intelligence of its own. He created a dynamo through which it would work, after years of patience and loving absorption in his work. Now this power lights the world, for it is harnessed and directed.

Man must harness and direct thought. Fear is as dangerous as uncontrolled electrical forces. Words and thoughts must be handled with wisdom and understanding. The imagination is man's workshop, and an imagination running wild and building-up fear pictures is just about as safe as riding a bucking broncho.

We were born and brought up in an age of doubt and fear. We were told that the age of miracles was over and to expect the worst. An optimistic person was laughed at. A bright remark was—"A pessimist is a person who lives with an optimist." "Eat the speckled apples first," was thought the height of wisdom. They did not seem to realize that by following this advice they would never catch up with the good apples, for they would be speckled, too, by the time they were reached.

What a beautiful world this would be if all anxiety and fear were blotted out. These twins, anxiety and worry, have made men slaves and are destroyers of health, wealth and happiness.

There is only one way of getting rid of fear—and that is, to transmute it into faith; for fear is the opposite of faith. We must trust the God within to guide, protect and provide. We must trust the science of mind, the power of thought and the power of the word. We must have faith, for faith registers the idea in the subconscious mind. When an idea is once registered in the subconscious, it must objectify.

How are we to get rid of this anxiety, which we might call "anti-faith"? The only way to neutralize it is to walk up to the thing you are afraid of.

There was a man who had lost all his money. He was living in very poor quarters and all the people around him were poor and he was afraid to spend the little he had. All he had was about five dollars. He had tried to get work but everyone had turned him down. He awoke one morning to face another day of lack and disappointment, when the idea (or hunch) came to him to go to the horse show. It took about all he had but he was fired with the idea of being with rich and successful people again. He was tired of his limited surroundings. He fearlessly spent the money for a ticket to the Horse Show. There he met an old friend, who said: "Hello, Jim! Where have you been all this time?" Before the Show was over the old friend gave him a wonderful position in his firm. His hunch and fearless attitude toward money had put him in a new vibration of success. Form the habit of making giant swings into faith. You will receive marvelous returns.

As has already been noted, we look with amazement at the people in the circus performing their remarkable feats. These people have the faith that they can perform these acts, and see themselves doing them. You cannot accomplish anything you cannot see yourself accomplishing. These difficult feats are all a matter of poise and balance. Your success and happiness depend upon your poise and balance.

Trusting God is like walking a slack wire. Doubt and fear cause you to lose your balance and fall off into lack and limitation. Like the circus performer—it takes practice. No matter how many times you fail, try it again. Soon you will acquire the habit of poise and balance. Then the world is yours. You will walk joyfully into your kingdom. The circus performers all seem to love their work, no matter how difficult. The band plays, the people applaud and they smile, but remember they were trained without the music and applause.

Man, free from worry and fear, asks with thanksgiving, and his good is given him.

Chapter 9 - VICTORY AND FULFILLMENT

Victory and fulfillment are two wonderful words and since we realize that words and thoughts are a form of radioactivity, we carefully choose the words we wish to see crystallized.

Life is a crossword puzzle; the right word gives you the answer. Many people are rattling off destructive words in their conversation. We hear them say: "I'm broke! I'm sick!" Remember by your words you are justified and by your words you are condemned. You are condemned by them because they do not return void. Change your words and you change your world, for your word is your world. You choose your food and the world is now calorie conscious. People no longer eat buckwheat cakes, beefsteak, potatoes, pie and three cups of coffee for breakfast. To keep down weight they eat dry toast and orange juice. This is tremendous discipline, but they are working for results. Why not try a diet of the right words—for you are literally eating your words. That is the value of the affirmation. You are deliberately building up a constructive idea in your consciousness. Your consciousness may be crammed and jammed with destructive ideas, but continually making a statement of Truth will dissolve these negative thought-forms. These thought-forms have been built up from your own vain imaginings.

Perhaps as a child you were taught that life was hard, happiness fleeting, and that the world was cold and unfriendly. These ideas were impressed upon your subconscious, and you found things just as they were predicted. With a knowledge of Truth all these external pictures may be changed, for they are only pictures, which change as your subconscious beliefs change.

When I tell people about the power of the word, and that words and thoughts are a form of radioactivity and do not return void, they say: "Oh, is it as easy as that?" Many people like things difficult and hard to understand.

A woman came to me filled with fears and forebodings. She said for years she had been pursued by the fear that even if she should receive the desire of her heart, something would happen to spoil it. I gave her the statement: "The Divine Plan of your life is a perfect idea in Divine Mind, incorruptible and indestructible, and cannot be spoiled in any way." A great load was lifted from her consciousness. For the first time in years she had a feeling of joy and freedom. Know the Truth and the Truth gives you a sense of freedom, soon then comes the actual freedom on the external.

This Supreme Intelligence is what man becomes one with, when he speaks the word. This Supreme Intelligence awaits man's direction, but It must have right of way, It must not be limited.

Divine Activity in your body brings health. There is only one disease—congestion, and one cure—circulation. Congestion and stagnation are the same thing. People say they "have got into a rut." A new idea will take them out of a rut. We must get out of the rut of negative thinking.

The word 'enthusiasm' in the dictionary is defined, "to be inspired or possessed by a god." Enthusiasm is divine fire and kindles enthusiasm in others. To be a good salesman you must be enthusiastic about the articles you are selling. If you are bored with your business or uninterested, the fires go out, and no one else will be interested.

A woman came to me for success in business. She said, "I have a shop but it is usually empty. I do not bother to open it until late in the day, what's the use?" I replied, "There is indeed no use so long as you feel the way you do. You are keeping people away. Become enthusiastic over what you have to sell. Be enthusiastic about yourself. Be enthusiastic about the God-power within you, and get up early to open your shop and be ready for the big crowd."

By this time she was all wound up with divine expectancy. She dashed down to her shop as early as possible and people were waiting outside and poured in all day.

People often say to me, "Treat my business." I say, "No, I will treat you, for YOU are your business." Your quality of thought penetrates every article for sale and all the conditions connected with it.

We are having a renaissance, a new birth, teaching a universal principle without creed or ceremony. We see members of all religions, denominations, coming into this Truth movement. It does not take them away from their churches. In fact, many clergymen are now teaching what the metaphysicians are teaching. We are learning to "Pray aright," and have understanding faith.

A woman told me of an answered prayer. Her son wrote her that he was going to southern California on a business trip in his car. She read in the morning paper of a flood, and she immediately spoke the word for divine protection. She had a great feeling of security; she knew he would be protected. She soon heard from him, saying some business had interfered with his leaving, so he was detained. If he had left when he had expected, he would have been in the flood district.

We become divinely enthusiastic about our answered prayers, which we call "demonstrations," for it means that we have demonstrated the truth and have been set free from some limitation.

The 24th Psalm is one of the most enthusiastic of the many Psalms of praise and thanksgiving.

"Lift up your heads, oh ye gates and be ye lifted up ye everlasting doors; and the King of Glory shall come in. Who is this King of glory, the Lord strong and mighty, the Lord mighty in battle."

The gates and doors symbolize man's consciousness. As you are lifted up in consciousness, you contact the superconscious, the God within, and the King of glory comes in. This King of glory lifts your burdens and fights your battles, solves your problems.

The average person has a difficult time LETTING the King of glory come in. Doubt, fear and apprehension keep the doors and gates locked against your good.

A student told me of a situation which she attracted by negative thinking. She had been invited to a gathering of old and valued friends. It was of the utmost importance for her to be there. She was so anxious to go, she said to herself repeatedly, "Oh, I hope nothing happens to interfere." The day of the reception arrived and she awoke with a terrific headache. At one time she had been subject to these headaches, going to bed for several days, but she had not had one for many years. Her doubts and fears had attracted this disappointment. She called me up and said, "Will you please speak the word that I will be well by evening to go to the reception?" I replied, "Why, of course, nothing can interfere with God's perfect plan." So, I spoke the word.

Later, she told me of her miracle. She said in spite of the way she felt, she prepared to go. She cleaned her jewelry, got her dress ready to wear, and attended to every detail, though she felt scarcely able to move. Very late in the afternoon, she said she had a peculiar sensation as of a fog lifting in her consciousness, and she was perfectly well. She went to the reception and had a wonderful time. I believe that the healing might have come more quickly had she not said, "I want to be well by tonight." We are continually limiting ourselves by our words, so not until night was she perfectly well. "By your word you are justified and by your word you are condemned."

I knew a man who was the center of attraction wherever he went, because he was always enthusiastic about something. Whether it was about shoes, clothes or a haircut, he enthused others into buying the

198

same things. He did not gain anything material by it, he was just naturally enthusiastic. Someone has said, "If you want to be interesting to others, be interested in something." An interested person is an enthusiastic person. We often hear people say: "Do tell me what you're interested in."

Many people are without vital interests and are hungry to hear what other people are doing. They are usually the ones who keep the radio turned on from early morning till late at night. They must be entertained every minute. Their own affairs do not hold enough interest.

A woman once said to me: "I love other people's affairs." She lived on gossip. Her conversation consisted of, "I was told," "I was given to understand," or "I heard." It is needless to say she is now paying her Karmic debt. A great unhappiness has overtaken her and everyone knows about her affairs. It is dangerous to neglect your own affairs and to take an idle curiosity in what others are doing. We should all be busily engaged in perfecting ourselves, but take a kindly interest in others.

Make the most of your disappointments by transmuting them into happy surprises. Transmute all failure into success. Transmute all unforgiveness into forgiveness, all injustice into justice. You will be kept busy enough perfecting your own life; you won't have time to run other people's affairs.

With divine enthusiasm I bless what I have, and look with wonder at their increase.

FLORENCE
SCOVEL SHINN

the
GAME of LIFE
AND   MP3
HOW TO
PLAY IT

by Florence Scovel Shinn (Author),
Dixie Glassman (Narrator)

Online at:
www.bnpublishing.net

Made in the USA
Charleston, SC
15 December 2009